A Sourcebook about Christian Death

The Sourcebook Series:

An Advent Sourcebook

A Christmas Sourcebook

A Lent Sourcebook: The Forty Days (two volumes)

A Triduum Sourcebook (three volumes)

An Easter Sourcebook: The Fifty Days

A Baptism Sourcebook

A Marriage Sourcebook

A Reconciliation Sourcebook

A Sourcebook about Christian Death

A Sourcebook about Liturgy

A Sourcebook about Music

A Sourcebook about Christian Death

Compiled by
Virginia Sloyan

Art by
Linda Ekstrom

LITURGY
TRAINING
PUBLICATIONS

Acknowledgments

I am indebted to Lisa Tarker, not only for her fine contributions to this book but just as much for her help in shaping its contents. My gratitude also to Gabe Huck and Peter Mazar for their contributions to the assembly of texts, to other friends and family members for their research and to all who have graciously consented to our use of copyrighted material.

Virginia Sloyan

Every effort has been made to determine the ownership of all texts and to make proper arrangements for their use. Any oversight that may have occurred, if brought to our attention, will gladly be corrected in future editions. A complete list of the acknowledgments will be found in the endnotes.

Scripture texts used in this work, unless otherwise noted, are taken from the *New American Bible with Revised New Testament,* copyright © 1986 Confraternity of Christian Doctrine, and are used by license of copyright owner. All rights reserved. No part of the *New American Bible with Revised New Testament* may be reproduced in any form without permission in writing from the copyright owner.

Series design format: Michael Tapia

Copyright © 1989, Archdiocese of Chicago. All rights reserved. Liturgy Training Publications, 1800 North Hermitage Avenue, Chicago IL 60622-1101; 1-800-933-1800; fax 1-800-933-7094; e-mail orders@ltp.org.

05 04 03 02 01 00 99 98   8 7 6 5 4 3

Printed in the United States of America.

ISBN 0-929650-09-3

Contents

Introduction: Being with Death

No one picking up this book is without strong convictions and feelings about death. We know what we know and we feel what we feel, and most of us are cautious above giving up those faithful possessions of mind and heart for strange, new ones.

A Sourcebook about Christian Death is not directed primarily to changing the long-held attitudes of its readers toward death. Many, in fact, will delight to see favorite lines from scripture and poems that have played a part in their own formation. But the book does suggest another kind of change.

"Here," it says, "read these pages slowly. Don't be afraid of death. Deny neither its existence nor your own grief surrounding it. Avail yourself of death's company—through the words of ordinary people and artists, Jewish and Christian prayers, Bible passages, the witness of martyrs, the songs and hymns of believers. Let the prospect of death and resurrection in the Lord Jesus Christ, a prospect you share with all his followers, cast a light on all your days."

This book is to be read gently, lovingly, as one would read a cherished letter. It can serve a variety of functions, some of which exist in the minds of its editors, the rest in the creative imaginations of its readers. The book is intended as a kind of treasury, beckoning people who are dying and people who are mourning and people who are preparing rituals. All may find nourishment for mind and heart and body. Perhaps all of the authors represented here knew what Annie Dillard meant when she wrote: "Write as if you were dying. At the same time, assume you write for an audience consisting solely of terminal patients. That is, after all, the case."

Sourcebooks of this kind are often sought out for specific events: a funeral, wake, memorial Mass, family anniversary. The pages are then flipped through hurriedly, if other duties press, in an effort to find just the right poem, scripture selection, prose excerpt.

Two cautions must be noted here: that those who prepare liturgy and its music and its homilies take pains to learn all they can about the person who has died before choosing any words from these pages, and that all services reflect the communal nature of the life and death of Christians, even though many of the selections herein do not.

Those who mourn may wish to use this book through the traditional mourning time of 30 days, reading each day one of the sections (either in order through the book or at random). Finding one hymn, one psalm and one prayer to go with the reading of the texts can make of this a daily ritual of morning or evening prayer.

The book is also about November and can be used in much the same way during those 30 days. This is the time when the season and the liturgy ponder last things. In November or at another time, the book can serve one person or a group, in the latter case sparking good discussions and further collections of poems and prayers and other texts.

Those who immerse themselves in these pages will find that some passages contradict others, that secular selections are often stronger than religious ones, that the choice of certain lines over much better-known ones is a mystery to them. That just may turn the book into an even better tool for dialogue!

The collection is not free of exclusive language, and that is a pity. Wherever changes (words or structures) could be made, they were made. But generally selections were chosen because of their content, style and intrinsic aptness, and this basis of choice, on occasion, meant that inclusivity of language was sacrificed.

Grant us wisdom, Lord, to live at ease in death's presence, not to fear it but to face it as your will for us.

Virginia Sloyan

SING with all the saints in glory,
Sing the resurrection song!
Death and sorrow, earth's dark story,
To the former days belong.
All around the clouds are breaking,
Soon the storms of time shall cease;
In God's likeness, we awaken,
Knowing everlasting peace.

O what glory, far exceeding
All that eye has yet perceived!
Holiest hearts for ages pleading,
Never that full joy conceived.
God has promised, Christ prepares it,
There on high our welcome waits;
Ev'ry humble spirit shares it,
Christ has passed the eternal gates.

Life eternal! heav'n rejoices:
Jesus lives who once was dead;
Shout with joy, O deathless voices!
Child of God, lift up your head!
Patriarchs from distant ages,
Saints all longing for their heaven,
Prophets, psalmists, seers, and sages,
All await the glory giv'n.

Life eternal! O what wonders
Crowd on faith; what joy unknown,
When, amidst earth's closing thunders,
Saints shall stand before the throne!
O to enter that bright portal,
See that glowing firmament,
Know, with you, O God immortal,
"Jesus Christ whom you have sent!"

William Irons
Nineteenth century

THROUGH art, we are able to break bread with the dead, and without communion with the dead a fully human life is impossible.

W. H. Auden

SO we look again at our foreparents and realize that this is living by faith and by love. People who live this way are seeking a homeland, go to a homeland, bring in and embrace a homeland. These crazy, wild sojourners desire a better country than the secure, legalistic land of security. They desire a better country, that is, a heavenly one. God has already prepared for them a city. What a wild company we belong to. I mean, do you understand? These are our foreparents. These are the founders of our faith. These are the old alumni. These are the ones who established, with their sweat and tears, the "institution." They are wild people, persecuted people, going out, not-knowing-where-they're-going people. These are our foreparents we remember.

Vincent Harding

JERUSALEM, my happy home,
When shall I with you be?
When shall my sorrows have an end?
Your joys when shall I see?

Your saints are crowned with glory great;
They see God face to face;
They triumph still, they still rejoice:
In that most holy place.

There David stands with harp in hand
As master of the choir:
Ten thousand times that we were blest
That might this music hear.

There Magdalene has left her tears,
And cheerfully does sing
With blessed saints, whose harmony
In ev'ry street does ring.

Jerusalem, Jerusalem,
God grant that I may see
Your endless joy, and of the same
Partaker ever be!

F.B.P.
Sixteenth century

O NE of the tasks of the church, in its liturgical life as well as in its formal education, is to recall the history of humanity in a different way than is usual in secular society. History is usually the story of conquerors, where greatness is measured in wars won and peoples subdued. Will Cuppy had this in mind when he wrote of Alexander III of Macedonia: "He is known as Alexander the Great because he killed more people of more different kinds than any other man of his time." The church, on the other hand, remembers a different sort of hero. The liturgical year commemorates saints who suffered unjustly, or who alleviated or prevented the suffering of others. July 4 is now the feast day of Isabel (Elizabeth) of Portugal, who prevented several wars by convincing her royal relatives to negotiate rather than set their peasants to slaughtering each other. . . . Then there is Hugh of Lincoln, who refused to accept the office of prior until the king had housed and fully compensated every peasant who had been evicted in order to build the new monastery, and who alone faced down and quelled anti-Semitic lynch mobs, so that at times there were Jew-murdering riots in every major English city except his diocese of Lincoln. . . . Rather than see such people as human-interest sidebar stories in a history focused on the wielders of power, the liturgical calendar puts them in center stage of the history that matters.

Elaine Ramshaw

SINCE the fourth century various Eastern churches have commemorated a feast of all martyrs. By the sixth century this commemoration was celebrated at Rome. November 1 as the date for this celebration in the West seems to have originated in Ireland and/or Britain where it was seen as a "harvest feast" at the close of the liturgical year. In 844, Pope Gregory IV established this date for all the Roman church. Joined to the day was the commemoration of the dedication of the Pantheon as the church of St. Mary and All Martyrs.

Saint Andrew
Bible Missal

AS Jacob with travel was weary one day,
At night on a stone for a pillow he lay;
He saw in a vision a ladder so high,
That its foot was on earth and its top in the sky:

The ladder is long, it is strong and well-made,
Has stood hundreds of years and is not yet decayed;
Many millions have climbed it and reached Sion's hill,
And thousands by faith are climbing it still:

Come, let us ascend! all may climb it who will;
For the angels of Jacob are guarding it still:
And remember, each step that by faith we pass o'er,
Some prophet or martyr hath trod it before:

And when we arrive at the haven of rest,
We shall hear the glad words, "Come up hither you blest,
Here are regions of light, here are mansions of bliss."
O, who would not climb such a ladder as this:

Alleluia to Jesus, who died on the tree
And has raised up a ladder of mercy for me,
English folk song   And has raised up a ladder of mercy for me.

ONCE people used to go to our cemeteries on Sundays and walk between the graves, singing beautiful hymns and spreading sweet-smelling incense. It set your heart at rest; it allayed the painful fears of inevitable death. It was almost as though the dead were smiling from under their grey mounds: "It's all right. . . . Don't be afraid."

But nowadays, if a cemetery is kept up, there's a sign hanging there: "Owners of graves! Keep this place tidy on penalty of a fine." But more often they just roll them flat with bull-dozers, to build sports grounds and parks.

Alexander Solzhenitsyn

WE await Elijah's arrival, we ask God to inspire us by the example of all the martyrs for truth and faith, the witnesses to God in darkness and suffering. Out of the depths of affliction their testimony becomes a song of hope and faith in justice and of trust in the common bond that unites peoples.

Passover liturgy

COME, ye thankful people, come,
Raise the song of harvest home:
All is safely gathered in,
Ere the winter storms begin;
God, our Maker, does provide
For our wants to be supplied;
Come to God's own temple, come,
Raise the song of harvest home.

All the world is God's own field,
Fruit unto his praise to yield;
Wheat and tares together sown,
Unto joy or sorrow grown;
First the blade, and then the ear,
Then the full corn shall appear:
Grant, O harvest Lord, that we
Wholesome grain and pure may be.

For the Lord our God shall come,
And shall take his harvest home;
From his field shall in that day
All offenses purge away;
Give the angels charge at last
In the fire the tares to cast,
But the fruitful ears to store
In his garner evermore.

Even so, Lord, quickly come
To your final harvest home;
Gather all your people in,
Free from sorrow, free from sin;
There, for ever purified,
In your presence to abide:
Come, with all your angels, come,
Raise the glorious harvest home.

Henry Alford
Nineteenth century

R EQUIEM aeternam dona eis Domine:
et lux perpetua luceat eis.

Eternal rest grant unto them, O Lord,
and let perpetual light shine upon them.

Catholic funeral rite

T HERE is a time for everything, for all things under the sun:
a time to be born and a time to die, a time to laugh and a
time to cry, a time to dance and a time to mourn, a time to
seek and a time to lose, a time to forget and a time to
remember.

This day in sacred convocation we remember those who
gave us life. We remember those who enriched our lives
with love and beauty, kindness and compassion, thoughtful-
ness and understanding. We renew our bonds to those who
have gone the way of all the earth. As we reflect upon those
whose memory moves us this day, we seek consolation, and
the strength and the insight born of faith.

Tender as a parent with a child, the Lord is merciful. God
knows how we are fashioned, remembers that we are dust.
Our days are as grass; we flourish as a flower in the field. The
wind passes over it and it is gone, and no one can recognize
where it grew. But the Lord's compassion for us, the Lord's
righteousness to children's children, remain, age after age,
unchanging.

Jewish prayer

A general commemoration of all the faithful departed was
celebrated by the churches of the East on the Saturday
before Lent. In the eighth century a similar commemoration
was found in many monasteries of the Western Church. In
998, St. Odilo of Cluny established November 2 as an
annual commemoration of the dead in all the monasteries of
the Cluniac federation. The celebration was spread by the
new orders of the tenth- and eleventh-century Gregorian
reform. It was adopted at Rome in the fourteenth century.

Saint Andrew
Bible Missal

G OD redeems our life from the grave. May we all be charitable in deed and in thought, in memory of those we love who walk the earth no longer.

May we live unselfishly, in truth and love and peace, so that we will be remembered as a blessing, as we this day lovingly remember those whose lives endure as a blessing.

May God remember the soul of my mother who has gone to her eternal home. In loving testimony to her life I pledge charity to help perpetuate ideals important to her. Through such deeds, and through prayer and memory, is her soul bound up in the bond of life. May I prove myself worthy of the gift of life and the many other gifts with which she blessed me. May these moments of meditation link me more strongly with her memory and with our entire family. May she rest eternally in dignity and peace. Amen.

May God remember the soul of my father who has gone to his eternal home. In loving testimony to his life I pledge charity to help perpetuate ideals important to him. Through such deeds, and through prayer and memory, is his soul bound up in the bond of life. May I prove myself worthy of the gift of life and the many other gifts with which he blessed me. May these moments of meditation link me more strongly with his memory and with our entire family. May he rest eternally in dignity and peace. Amen.

Jewish prayer

L ORD Jesus Christ,
by your own three days in the tomb,
you hallowed the graves of all who believe in you
and so made the grave a sign of hope
that promises resurrection
even as it claims our mortal bodies.

Grant that our brothers and sisters may sleep
   here in peace
until you awaken them to glory,
for you are the resurrection and the life.
Then they will see you face to face
and in your light will see light
and know the splendor of God,
for you live and reign for ever and ever.

*Order of Christian
Funerals*

WE still pray
   We still sing
We still dream of the day
when the birds will return
and the flowers
and our lost loved ones

We still live with the belief
that love and gentleness
and faith
will blossom forth one day
like roses in winter

We still believe that God
will be born again in our land
as we prepare the stable
of our hearts for the birth
of a new people

*To Guatemalan
refugees in Mexico
from Salvadoran
refugees in Honduras*

C OME, brothers and sisters, let us consider the dust and ashes of which we were formed. What is the reality of our present life and what shall we become tomorrow? In death where is the poor and where the rich? Where is the slave and where the master? They are all ashes. The beauty of the countenance has withered, and the strength of youth has been cut down by death. . . . All has withered as the grass of the field and has vanished. Come . . . let us fall on our knees in humble prayer before Christ.

Orthodox liturgy

T HE sight of a singing, swinging skeleton is a familiar decorative figure during *Días de los Muertos*. In fact, skeletons engaged in all types of daily activity such as performing the duties of a police officer, playing in a band, riding a bicycle or driving a bus are common. Though each skeleton has his or her own personality there is one thing that is recognizable in all of them—a distinct grin. These "grins" show the human, ironical nature of the skeleton. Perhaps the skeletons are amused that it is the living who really suffer, struggling to stay alive. *Días de los Muertos* reminds the living that death is a prelude to resurrection. In this way death, portrayed by the skeleton, is seen also as the beginning of life. . . .

When the Spanish laid claim to Mexico's soil, the lives of the Mexican Indians were completely disrupted. Those Indians engaged in mask wearing to transport them beyond the hardships to which they were subjected by the Spanish invasion. In a sense, by wearing the masks they could cover their very souls and so be transformed into someone else in a different, more positive situation. The skull-mask represented the Indians' belief that death was just part of the cycle of life. After the Spanish arrived and introduced the Indians to Catholicism, the skull took on the added meanings associated with the Catholic feast of All Souls Day. The skull-mask was and is occasionally worn with an accompanying full skeleton suit of clothing. It is *always* worn in the spirit of possibilities and of the unknown.

Días de los Muertos

L ORD our God,
the death of our brother/sister N.
recalls our human condition
and the brevity of our lives on earth.
But for those who believe in your love
death is not the end,
nor does it destroy the bonds
that you forge in our lives.
We share the faith of your Son's disciples
and the hope of the children of God.
Bring the light of Christ's resurrection
to this time of testing and pain
as we pray for N. and for those who love him/her,
through Christ our Lord.

*Order of Christian
Funerals*

I T falsifies the Christian message to present and to preach
Christianity as essentially life-affirming—without refer-
ring this affirmation to the death of Christ and therefore to the
very fact of death; to pass over in silence the fact that for
Christianity death is not only the end, but indeed, the very
reality of *this world.* But to "comfort" people and reconcile
them with death by making this world a meaningless scene
of an individual preparation for death is also to falsify it. For
Christianity proclaims that Christ died for the life of the
world, and not for an "eternal rest" from it.

Alexander
Schmemann

L ET us turn to Christ Jesus with confidence and faith in the
power of his cross and resurrection:

Risen Lord, pattern of our life for ever:
Lord, have mercy.

Promise and image of what we shall be:
Lord, have mercy.

Son of God who came to destroy sin and death:
Lord, have mercy.

Word of God who delivered us from the fear of death:
Lord, have mercy.

Crucified Lord, forsaken in death, raised in glory:
Lord, have mercy.

Lord Jesus, gentle Shepherd who bring rest to our souls,
give peace to N. for ever:
Lord, have mercy.

Lord Jesus, you bless those who mourn and are in pain. Bless
N.'s family and friends who gather around him/her today:
Lord, have mercy.

Order of Christian Funerals

A ND concerning the resurrection of the dead, have you
not read what was said to you by God, "I am the God of
Abraham, the God of Isaac, and the God of Jacob"? God is
not the God of the dead but of the living.

Matthew 22:31–32

I heard a voice from heaven say, "Write this: Blessed are the
dead who die in the Lord from now on." "Yes," said the
Spirit, "let them find rest from their labors, for their works
accompany them."

Revelation 14:13

H ERE lie I, Martin Elginbrodde:
Have mercy on my soul, Lord God,
As I would do, were I Lord God
and you were Martin Elginbrodde.

Epitaph in Elgin Cathedral

KEEP death and judgment always in your eye.
None's fit to live but who is fit to die.
New England epitaph

STRANGER, call this not a place
Of Fear and Gloom.
To me it is a pleasant Spot,
    It is my Husband's tomb.
North Dakota epitaph

SACRED to the memory of Amos Fortune,
Who was born free in Africa,
a slave in America,
he purchased liberty,
professed Christianity,
lived reputably,
and died hopefully.
November 17, 1801, Aet. 91.
New Hampshire epitaph

THIS body sleeps in dust
    Immortal joys await the host
In perfect beauty may it rise
When Gabriel's trumpet shakes the skies.
Long Island epitaph

WILL the circle be unbroken,
By and by, Lord, by and by?
There's a better home a-waiting.
In the sky, Lord, in the sky.

American folk song

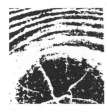

MARGARET, are you grieving
Over Goldengrove unleaving?
Leaves, like the things of man, you
With your fresh thoughts care for, can you?
Ah! as the heart grows older
It will come to such sights colder
By and by, nor spare a sigh
Though worlds of wanwood leafmeal lie;
And yet you *will* weep and know why.
Now no matter, child, the name:
Sorrow's springs are the same.
Nor mouth had, no nor mind, expressed
What heart heard of, ghost guessed:
It is the blight man was born for,
It is Margaret you mourn for.

Gerard Manley
Hopkins
Nineteenth century

THE span of Sarah's life was 127 years. She died in
Kiriatharba (that is, Hebron) in the land of Canaan, and
Abraham performed the customary mourning rites for her.
Then he left the side of his dead one and addressed the
Hittites: "Although I am a resident alien among you, sell me
from your holdings a piece of property for a burial ground,
that I may bury my dead wife."

Thus Ephron's field in Machpelah, facing Mamre, together
with its cave and all the trees anywhere within its limits, was
conveyed to Abraham by purchase in the presence of all the
Hittites who sat on Ephron's town council. After this transac-
tion, Abraham buried his wife Sarah in the cave of the field of
Machpelah, facing Mamre (that is, Hebron) in the land of
Canaan. Thus the field with its cave was transferred from the
Hittites to Abraham as a burial place.

Genesis 23:1–4,
17–20

THEN Moses went up from the plains of Moab to Mount Nebo, the headland of Pisgah which faces Jericho, and the LORD showed him all the land. The LORD then said to Moses, "This is the land which I swore to Abraham, Isaac and Jacob that I would give to their descendants. I have let you feast your eyes upon it, but you shall not cross over." So there, in the land of Moab, Moses, the servant of the LORD, died as the LORD had said; and he was buried in the ravine opposite Beth-peor in the land of Moab, but to this day no one knows the place of his burial. Moses was 120 years old when he died, yet his eyes were undimmed and his vigor unabated. For 30 days the Israelites wept for Moses in the plains of Moab, till they had completed the period of grief and mourning for Moses.

Since then no prophet has arisen in Israel like Moses, whom the Lord knew face to face.

Deuteronomy
34:1–8, 10

AMERICAN Indian studies show that] the traditions of the women have, since time immemorial, been centered on continuance, just as those of the men have been centered on transitoriness. The most frequently occurring male themes and symbols from the oral tradition have been feathers, smoke, lightning bolts (sheet lightning is female), risk, and wandering. These symbols are all related in some way to the idea of the transitoriness of life and its wonders. The Kiowa death song (a male tradition that was widespread among Plain tribes) says, "I die, but you live forever, beautiful Earth you alone remain; wonderful Earth, you remain forever," telling the difference in the two traditions, male and female.

The male principle is transitory; it dies and is reconstituted. The female principle, which is immanent in hard substances (like the earth, minerals, crystals, and stones), wood, and water, is permanent; it remains. Male is breath, air, wind and projectile point; female controls, creates and "owns" breath, air and wind, bird and feather, and the hard substance from which the projectile point is shaped. Female is earth, sun, moon, sky, water in its multitudinous forms and its ever-generating cycle, corn, mother of the deer, mother of the gods, bringer of fire and light, and fire itself (which is why the women are its keepers among many if not most groups). He is what comes and goes; she is what continues, what stays.

When we shift our attention from the male, the transitory, to the female, the enduring, we realize that the Indians are not doomed to extinction but rather are fated to endure. What a redemptive, empowering realization that is! As the Cheyenne long have insisted, no people is broken until the heart of its women is on the ground. Then they are broken. Then will they die.

Paula Gunn Allen

T HE LORD took Abram outside and said: "Look up at the sky and count the stars, if you can. Just so . . . shall your descendants be." Abram put his faith in the LORD, who credited it to him as an act of righteousness.

Genesis 15:5–6

T HE greatest problem is not how to continue but how to exalt our existence. The cry for a life beyond the grave is presumptuous, if there is no cry for eternal life prior to our descending to the grave. Eternity is not perpetual future but perpetual presence. God has planted in us the seed of eternal life. The world to come is not only a hereafter but also a *herenow*.

Our greatest problem is not how to continue but how to return. "How can I repay unto the Lord all his bountiful dealings with me?" (Psalm 116:12) When life is an answer, death is a home-coming. "Precious in the sight of the Lord is the death of his saints." (Psalm 116:15) . . . This is the meaning of death: the ultimate self-dedication to the divine. Death so understood will not be distorted by the craving for immortality, for this act of giving away is reciprocity on our part for God's gift of life. For the pious . . . it is a privilege to die.

Abraham Joshua
Heschel

IF I die,
leave the balcony open.

The little boy is eating oranges.
(From my balcony I can see him.)

The reaper is harvesting the wheat.
(From my balcony I can hear him.)

If I die,
leave the balcony open!   Federico García Lorca

THERE is a sense in which the Christian life is supposed to be the rehearsal for death. And it is not a morbid sense. If a death that is a free completion of life and a surrendering of oneself to the Father is possible in Jesus Christ and for his followers, this gives a personal dignity that enhances the whole of life, because it makes the purposefulness and freedom of a human life real and meaningful. If death must necessarily be a passive experience of being taken over by the inevitable in spite of oneself, then life is after all absurd and freedom just a cruel jest.   Monika Hellwig

O God, our help in ages past,
Our hope for years to come,
Our shelter from the stormy blast,
And our eternal home:

Under the shadow of your throne
Your saints have dwelt secure;
Sufficient is your arm alone,
And our defense is sure.

Before the hills in order stood
Or earth received its frame,
From everlasting you are God,
To endless years the same.

A thousand ages in your sight
Are like an evening gone,
Short as the watch that ends the night
Before the rising sun.

Time, like an ever-rolling stream,
Soon bears us all away;
We fly forgotten, as a dream
Dies at the op'ning day.

Our God, our help in ages past,
Our hope for years to come,
Isaac Watts   Still be our guard while troubles last
Eighteenth century   And our eternal home.

L ORD, you have been a home for us,
For one generation after another.
Before the mountains were born,
   Before you gave birth to the continents,
   All through the ages you were God.
You turn everyone back into dust;
   You say, "Return, you mortal creatures!"
For in your eyes a thousand years
   Are like yesterday when it is gone,
   Like keeping watch for a night.
Our life begins in sleep;
   At dawn we sprout like grass.
At dawn we blossom and sprout;
   At evening we dry up and wither away.

For we are destroyed by your anger.
  And quickly dispatched by your rage.
You bring out our sins where you can see them;
  Your presence lights up our shameful secrets.
Every day we feel your wrath;
  We finish our years with sighing.
Our lives may go on for seventy years,
  Or even for eighty, if we are strong;
    But those years are nothing but work and pain.
Who understands your mighty anger,
  The rage that make us afraid of you?
Teach us how to plan our days,
  And let our conduct be wise.
Repent, O Lord! How long will this last?
  Be gracious to us, your servants.
Kindly care for us each morning;
  All our lives let us sing for joy.
Delight us as long as you have oppressed us,
  As many years as we have seen trouble.
Let your work be plain to your servants,
  And show our children your splendor.
Let our God's kindness rest upon us,
  And let the work we have done endure.
    What our hands have done—let it endure!   Psalm 90

A wisp of spring cloud
drifting apart from the rest . . .
slowly evaporates.   Haiku

REMEMBER also your Creator in the days of your youth, before the evil days come, and the years draw nigh, when you will say, "I have no pleasure in them"; before the sun and the light and the moon and the stars are darkened and the clouds return after the rain; in the day when the keepers of the house tremble, and the strong are bent, and the grinders cease because they are few, and those that look through the windows are dimmed, and the doors on the street are shut; when the sound of the grinding is low, and one rises up at the voice of a bird, and all the daughters of song are brought low; they are afraid also of what is high, and terrors are in the way; the almond tree blossoms, the grasshopper drags itself along and desire fails; because someone goes to the eternal home, and the mourners go about the streets; before the silver cord is snapped, or the golden bowl is broken, or the pitcher is broken at the fountain, or the wheel broken at the cistern, and the dust returns to the earth as it was, and the spirit returns to God who gave it. Vanity of vanities, says the Preacher; all is vanity.

Ecclesiastes 12:1–8

ABOUT suffering they were never wrong,
The Old Masters: how well they understood
Its human position; how it takes place
While someone else is eating or opening a window or just
          walking dully along;
or, when the aged are reverently, passionately waiting
For the miraculous birth, there always must be
Children who did not specially want it to happen, skating
On a pond at the edge of the wood:
They never forgot
That even the dreadful martyrdom must run its course
Anyhow in a corner, some untidy spot
Where the dogs go on with their doggy life and
          the torturer's horse
Scratches its innocent behind on a tree.

In Brueghel's *Icarus,* for instance: how everything
     turns away
Quite leisurely from the disaster; the ploughman may
Have heard the splash, the forsaken cry,
But for him it was not an important failure; the sun shone
As it had to on the white legs disappearing into the green
Water; and the expensive delicate ship that must
     have seen
Something amazing, a boy falling out of the sky,
Had somewhere to get to and sailed calmly on.   W. H. Auden

THE name of God's life is love,
  and every time we gather around this altar
we celebrate a hanging—a death—
we celebrate the passage of Jesus,
the victory of God's life, love, over death itself.
Today we invite you to celebrate Aubry's passage, too,
in faith and confidence that Jesus is only the firstborn
        from the dead.
Aubry—a believer like us, close to us in the church,
among us in the church a servant, a priest for 20 years.
Aubry—human as we are, accepting the humanity and
        limits of us all,
loving as Jesus did especially the outcasts
        and the scorned.
Aubry—who gave thanks and smacked his lips at all
        good things of life,
and talked about the ham that we would eat when he had
        passed from us.
Aubry—a dreamer on whom life was hard because he
        saw the kingdom,
like Martin Luther King and all true followers of Jesus,
he had been to the mountaintop and he had seen the
        reign of God,
and he knew, as we all should know, that we have to
        change this world of ours
to make it fit for sisters and brothers.
All this we celebrate, as we pray and offer sacrifice
        for Aubry,
pledging ourselves to him in Christ—to believe and hope,
        to accept,
to give thanks, to dream and to take up the cross
        of dreamers.

Robert W. Hovda

MAGNIFIED and sanctified be the great name of God throughout the world which he hath created according to his will. May he establish his kingdom during the days of your life and during the life of all the house of Israel, speedily, yea, soon; and say ye, Amen.

May his great name be blessed for ever and ever.

Exalted and honored be the name of the Holy One, blessed be he, whose glory transcends, yea, is beyond all blessings and hymns, praises and consolations which are uttered in the world; and say ye, Amen.

May there be abundant peace from heaven, and life for us and for all Israel; and say ye, Amen.

May he who establisheth peace in the heavens, grant peace unto us and unto all Israel; and say ye, Amen.   Kaddish

COHN said Kaddish for one hundred souls whose names he had picked at random in a heavily thumbed copy of a Manhattan telephone directory he had snatched from the sea-battered *Rebekah Q.* He kept it for company in the cave as a sort of "Book of the Dead."

He often felt an urge to read all those names aloud. The Dead must be acknowledged if one respected life. He would say Kaddish at least once for everyone in the book, although, technically speaking, to do so one needed the presence of ten live Jews. Yet, since there were not ten in the world, there was no sin saying it via only one man. Who was counting?

God said nothing.

Cohn said Kaddish.

There's a legend in Midrash that Moses did not want to die despite his so-called old age. He was against it, respectfully, of course.

"Master of the World! Let me stay like a bird that flies on the four winds and gathers its food every day, and at eventide returns to the nest. Let me be like one of them!"

"With all due regard for services rendered," God said, "nothing doing. You're asking too much. That mixes everything up. First things first."

Cohn said Kaddish.

If we were bound to come to this dreadful end, why did the All-knowing God create us?

Some sages said: In order to reflect His light. He liked to know He was present.

Some said: In order to create justice on earth; at least to give it a try.

Cohn thought: He was the Author of the universe. Each man was a story unto himself, it seemed. He liked beginnings and endings. He enjoyed endings based on beginnings, and beginnings on endings. He liked to guess out endings and watch them go awry. At first He liked the juicy parts where people were torn between good and evil; but later the stories may have let Him down; how often, without seeming to try, the evil triumphed. It wasn't an effect; it was an embarrassing condition: His insufficient creation. Man was subtly conceived but less well executed. Body and soul hung badly together.

Maybe next time.

Bernard Malamud   Cohn said Kaddish.

A priest working with base communities explains why fear loses hold [at times of great danger]: "Anybody can die just walking around in El Salvador. The poor know they are going to die anyway, so it might as well be for a good reason."

The desire to live freely, to live meaningfully, robs death of its power. For some in El Salvador, a chosen death is preferable to mute submission to the murderous machinery of terror. It is a choice that promises liberation not only for oneself, but also for others.

It is a resurrecting choice, one that was made by Archbishop Oscar Romero, whose spirit still hovers over this land. Speaking two weeks before his murder, he said, "I have often been threatened with death, but as a Christian I do not believe in death without resurrection. If they kill me, I will rise in the Salvadoran people."

Mary Jo Leddy

W ITH a mother's strong love
you shelter us in your own shadow, Lord,
and you mourn as we do the death of this child.
Hold N. gently in your hand
and help us to await in joyful hope
the resurrection of the dead
and the life of the world to come.

Gabe Huck

A FTER a dozen years of death
even love wanders off, old faithful
dog tired of lying on stiff marble.

In any case you would not understand
this life, the plain white walls
& the books, a passion lost on you.

I do not know what forced your life
through iron years into a shape of giving—
an apple, squares of chocolate, a hand.

There should have been nothing left
after the mean streets, foaming washtubs,
the wild cries of births at home.

Never mind. It's crumbling in my hands,
too, what you gave. I've jumped from ledges
& landed oddly twisted, bleeding internally.

Thus I learn to remember your injuries—
your sudden heaviness as fine rain fell,
or your silence over the scraped bread board.

Finding myself in the end is finding you
& if you are lost in the folds of your silence
then I find only to lose with you those years

I stupidly flung off me like ragged clothes
when I was ashamed to be the child
of your child. I scrabble for them now

In dark closets because I am afraid.
I have forgotten so much. If I could meet you
again perhaps I could rejoin my own flesh

And not lose whatever you called love.
I could understand your silences & speak them
& you would be as present to me as your worn ring.

In the shadows I reach for the bucket of fierce dahlias
you bought without pricing, the coat you shook
free of its snow, the blouse that you ironed.

There's no love so pure it can thrive
without its incarnations. I would like to know you
Michele Murray   once again over your chipped cups brimming with tea.

S HALL we gather at the river,
Where bright angel feet have trod;
With its crystal tide forever
Flowing by the throne of God?

    Yes, we'll gather at the river,
    The beautiful, the beautiful river;
    Gathered with the saints at the river
    That flows by the throne of God.

On the margin of the river,
Washing up its silver spray,
We will walk and worship ever,
All the happy golden day.

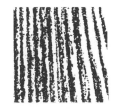

Soon we'll reach the shining river,
Soon our pilgrimage will cease,
Soon our happy hearts will quiver
With the melody of peace.   *American hymn*

H AIL holy Queen, mother of mercy,
hail, our life, our sweetness, and our hope.
To you we cry, the children of Eve;
to you we send up our sighs,
mourning and weeping in this land of exile.
Turn, then, most gracious advocate,
your eyes of mercy toward us;
lead us home at last
and show us the blessed fruit of your womb,
   Jesus:
O clement, O loving, O sweet Virgin Mary.   *Salve Regina*

WHEN the Lord shall again set Zion free—
Let us be as dreamers—
Then laughter will fill our mouths,
    And our tongues will shout for joy.
They will say among the nations,
    "The Lord has done great things for them!"
May the Lord do great things for us,
    And then may we rejoice!

Lord, bring back our exiles,
    Like streams to water the desert.
Those who sow with tears—
    May they gather the harvest with singing.
True, they may go out weeping,
    Bearing a pouch of seed;
But let them return with laughter,
Psalm 126   Bearing their sheaves of grain!

LIFE be in my speech,
Sense in what I say,
The bloom of cherries on my lips,
Till I come back again.

The love Christ Jesus gave
Be filling every heart for me,
The love Christ Jesus gave
Filling me for every one.

Traversing corries, traversing forests,
Traversing valleys long and wild.
The fair white Mary still uphold me,
The Shepherd Jesu be my shield,
The fair white Mary still uphold me,
Celtic prayer for
traveling   The shepherd Jesu be my shield.

OUR home is—Heaven. On earth we are like travelers staying at a hotel. When one is away, one is always thinking of going home.

John Vianney
Nineteenth century

NOW, when I can read my title clear
To mansions in the sky,
I'll bid farewell to every fear,
I will wipe my weeping eye.

Let others seek a place below
Where flames devour and forever roll;
Give me a home above the sky
Where I'll always live, I'll never die.

I'm a long time traveling here below,
I'm a long time a-traveling away from my home.
I'm a long time traveling here below,
Gonna lay this body down.

American hymn

FOR I am convinced that neither death, nor life, nor angels, nor principalities, nor present things, nor future things, nor powers, nor height, nor depth, nor any other creature will be able to separate us from the love of God in Christ Jesus, our Lord.

Romans 8:38–39

O LORD, you have probed me and you know me;
    you know when I sit and when I stand;
you understand my thoughts from afar.
My journeys and my rest you scrutinize,
    with all my ways you are familiar.
Even before a word is on my tongue,
    behold, O LORD, you know the whole of it.
Behind me and before, you hem me in
    and rest your hand upon me.
Such knowledge is too wonderful for me;
    too lofty for me to attain.

Where can I go from your spirit?
    from your presence where can I flee?
If I go up to the heavens, you are there;
    if I sink to the nether world, you are present there.
If I take the wings of the dawn,
    if I settle at the farthest limits of the sea,
Even there your hand shall guide me,
    and your right hand hold me fast.
If I say, "Surely the darkness shall hide me,
    and night shall be my light"—
For you darkness itself is not dark,
    and night shines as the day.
Darkness and light are the same.

Truly you have formed my inmost being;
    you knit me in my mother's womb,
I give you thanks that I am fearfully, wonderfully made;
    wonderful are your works.
My soul also you knew full well;
    nor was my frame unknown to you
When I was made in secret,
    when I was fashioned in the depths of the earth.

Your eyes have seen my actions;
   in your book they are all written;
   my days were limited before one of them existed.
How weighty are your designs, O God;
   how vast the sum of them!
Were I to recount them, they would outnumber the sands:
   did I reach the end of them, I should still be with you.   Psalm 139:1–18

I am weak but thou art strong;
Jesus, keep me from all wrong;
I'll be satisfied as long
As I walk, let me walk close to thee.

Through this world of toil and snares,
If I falter, Lord, who cares?
Who with me my burden shares?
None but thee, dear Lord, none but thee.

When my feeble life is o'er,
Time for me will be no more;
Guide me gently, safely o'er
To thy kingdom shore, to thy shore.

   Just a closer walk with thee,
   Grant it, Jesus, is my plea,
   Daily walking close to thee,
   Let it be, dear Lord, let it be.   American gospel song

H AIL Mary, full of grace,
the Lord is with you!
Blessed are you among women,
and blessed is the fruit of your womb,
    Jesus.
Holy Mary, Mother of God,
pray for us sinners,
now and at the hour of our death.

Traditional Catholic
prayer

M ARY moder, I you pray
To be owr help at domysday.

Old English carol

W HETHER [sickness] befalls us suddenly or develops
slowly, whether it turns out to be minor or chronic or
terminal, it seems always to take us by surprise. We know
intellectually that we are ultimately finite, but we seem
unprepared for the limits beyond which our bodily being
will not take us. Illness, therefore, deprives us of our pro-
jected future. In so doing, particularly if it is serious, it
threatens the destruction of faith and hope. We have placed
the most basic of unspoken trusts in our bodily life, and it has
betrayed us. Because of that betrayal we can no longer place
any real trust in the future. Hope requires that we project
that future as both possible and desirable. To the person who
is seriously ill, the future often seems to be neither. Time
shrinks to the eternal now, beyond which "be dragons" — in
the words of the ancient cartographers labeling the
unknown edges of the world. Beyond lies the ultimate
betrayal which is death, now recognized as certain even if
not immediate. The vision of death lurking within the experience of sickness seems to cut off the future absolutely, at
least from the experiential and imaginative viewpoint. With

the loss of the future goes the loss of meaning. That toward which life was lived, however unreflectively, no longer gives purpose and direction to the many relationships which constitute our world. In the face of the insuperable barrier of death, concealed behind the immediate limit of present sickness, life and its relationships threaten to become absurd. . . .

[Confronted with the inescapable prospect of my own death,] if not now then surely one day, my world has shattered into pieces at my feet. I never expected this, and now I do not know what to do. I suppose I should do something about it, about my person, about my loved ones, about my religion—but to tell you the truth, I do not know if I want to bother. What is the use? None of it makes any sense anymore anyway. The future is gone, meaning is gone. All the relationships which defined me—intrapersonal, inter-personal, and transpersonal—are in shambles. Heal that, if you will!

Jennifer Glen

I heard a fly buzz when I died;
The stillness in the room
Was like the stillness in the air
Between the heaves of storm.

The eyes around had wrung them dry,
And breaths were gathering firm
For that last onset, when the king
Be witnessed in the room.

I willed my keepsakes, signed away
What portion of me be
Assignable—and then it was
There interposed a fly,

With blue, uncertain, stumbling buzz,
Between the light and me;
And then the window failed, and then
I could not see to see.

Emily Dickinson
Nineteenth century

O
N the rough wet grass of the back yard my father and mother have spread quilts. We all lie there, my mother, my father, my uncle, my aunt, and I too am lying there. . . . All my people are larger bodies than mine. . . . One is an artist, he is living at home. One is a musician, she is living at home. One is my mother who is good to me. One is my father who is good to me. By some chance, here they are, all on this earth; and who shall ever tell the sorrow of being on this earth, lying, on quilts, on the grass, in a summer evening, among the sounds of night. May God bless my people, my uncle, my aunt, my mother, my good father, oh, remember them kindly in their time of trouble and in the hour of their taking away.

James Agee

F
ATHER,
you made us in your own image
and your son accepted death for our salvation.
Help us to keep watch in prayer at all times.
May we be free from sin when we leave this world
and rejoice in peace with you for ever.

Prayer for
a good death

J
ESUS, Mary, and Joseph,
I give you my heart and my soul.
Jesus, Mary, and Joseph,
    assist me in the hour of my death.
Jesus, Mary, and Joseph,
    may I die and rest in peace with you.

Traditional
Catholic prayer

M
AY God support us all the day long till the shades lengthen and the evening comes and the busy world is hushed and the fever of life is over and our work is done. Then in mercy may God give us a safe lodging and a holy rest and peace at the last.

John Henry Newman
Nineteenth century

O God, who broughtst me from the rest of last night
  Unto the joyous light of this day,
Be thou bringing me from the new light of this day
Unto the guiding light of eternity.
  Oh! from the new light of this day
  Unto the guiding light of eternity.   Celtic prayer

THERE was once a dervish who embarked upon a sea journey. As the other passengers in the ship came aboard one by one, they saw him and—as is the custom—asked him for a piece of advice. All the dervish would do was to say the same thing to each one of them: He seemed merely to be repeating one of those formulas, which each dervish makes the object of his attention from time to time. The formula was: "Try to be aware of death, until you know what death is." Few of the travelers felt particularly attracted to this admonition.

Presently a terrible storm blew up. The crew and the passengers alike fell upon their knees, imploring God to save the ship. They alternately screamed in terror, gave themselves up for lost, hoped wildly for succour. All this time the dervish sat quietly, reflective, reacting not at all to the movement and the scenes which surrounded him.

Eventually the buffeting stopped, the sea and sky were calm, and the passengers became aware how serene the dervish had been throughout the episode. One of them asked him: "Did you not realize that during this frightful tempest there was nothing more solid than a plank between us all and death?"

"Oh, yes, indeed," answered the dervish. "I knew that at sea it is always thus. I also realized, however, that I had often reflected when I was on land that, in the normal course of events, there is *even less* between us and death."   Tales of the Dervishes

A south wind blew gently, and thinking they had attained their objective, they weighed anchor and sailed along close to the coast of Crete. Before long an offshore wind of hurricane force called a "Northeaster" struck. Since the ship was caught up in it and could not head into the wind we gave way and let ourselves be driven. We passed along the sheltered side of an island named Cauda and managed only with difficulty to get the dinghy under control. They hoisted it aboard, then used cables to undergird the ship. Because of their fear that they would run aground on the shoal of Syrtis, they lowered the drift anchor and were carried along in this way. We were being pounded by the storm so violently that the next day they jettisoned some cargo, and on the third day with their own hands they threw even the ship's tackle overboard. Neither the sun nor the stars were visible for many days, and no small storm raged. Finally, all hope of our surviving was taken away.

Until the day began to dawn, Paul kept urging all to take some food. He said, "Today is the fourteenth day that you have been waiting, going hungry and eating nothing. I urge you, therefore, to take some food; it will help you survive. Not a hair of the head of anyone of you will be lost." When he said this, he took bread, gave thanks to God in front of them all, broke it, and began to eat. They were all encouraged, and took some food themselves. In all, there were two hundred seventy-six of us on the ship. After they had eaten enough, they lightened the ship by throwing the wheat into the sea.

Acts 27:13–20, 33–38

PROFESSOR Hans Jonas once wrote an essay in which he mused over the disposition of our generation to regard death as an awkward interruption of a play that was so pleasantly getting on very well. Human life has been increasingly brought under such managerial powers as to make death a cheat, a ludicrous interruption, an event for which an entire profession has conspired to cosmetize the dead and narcotize the survivors.

Joseph Sittler

SINCE in baptism the body was marked with the seal of the Trinity and became the temple of the Holy Spirit, Christians respect and honor the bodies of the dead and the places where they rest. Any customs associated with the preparation of the body of the deceased should always be marked with dignity and reverence and never with the despair of those who have no hope. Preparation of the body should include prayer, especially at those intimate moments reserved for family members. For the final disposition of the body, it is the ancient Christian custom to bury or entomb the bodies of the dead; cremation is permitted, unless it is evident that cremation was chosen for anti-Christian motives.

In countries or regions where an undertaker, and not the family or community, carries out the preparation and transfer of the body, the pastor and other ministers are to ensure that the undertakers appreciate the values and beliefs of the Christian community.

The family and friends of the deceased should not be excluded from taking part in the services sometimes provided by undertakers, for example, the preparation and laying out of the body.

Order of Christian Funerals

THE embalming of a corpse, the situation of the tomb, the funeral procession, are a consolation to the living rather than assistance to the dead. Yet it does not follow that the bodies of the dead are to be neglected or flung aside, especially not the bodies of holy and faithful persons, since these bodies were once the instruments and vessels used holily by these souls to do all their good works. A father's ring, his robe, or some other belonging is dear to those left behind in proportion to the affection borne toward this parent. The bodies of the dead are not to be uncared for in any way, since these bodies are dearer and nearer to us than any garment. These bodies are not ornaments or aids applied from without; they are of the very nature of human beings. . . . The care bestowed upon the burial of the body is no aid to salvation. It is merely an act of humanity regulated by affection. It is most proper that one should care for the corpse of a neighbor when that neighbor has died. If these offices are paid to the dead, even by those who do not believe in the resurrection of the body, how much more should they be paid by those who do believe in the resurrection on the last day? Thus these duties toward a body, which *Augustine* although dead is destined to rise again and to live through- *Fifth century* out eternity, are in a way a testimony of faith in that belief.

F ORMERLY, they used to bring food to the house of mourn-
ing, the rich in baskets of gold and silver, the poor in baskets of willow twigs; and the poor felt ashamed. There- fore, a law was instituted that all should use baskets of willow twigs. . . .

Formerly they used to bring out the deceased for burial, the rich on a tall state bed, ornamented and covered with rich coverlets, the poor on a plain bier (or box); and the poor felt ashamed. Therefore, a law was instituted that all should be brought out on a plain bier. . . .

Formerly the expense of the burial was harder to bear by the family than the death itself, so that sometimes they fled to escape the expense. This was so until Rabban Gamaliel insisted that he be buried in a plain linen shroud instead of costly garments. And since then we follow the principle of *Talmud* burial in a simple manner.

W HEN life sinks apace, and death is in view,
This word of his grace shall comfort us through:
The Southern No fearing or doubting with Christ on our side,
Harmony We hope to die shouting, the Lord will provide.

I am not resigned to the shutting away of loving hearts in
the hard ground.
So it is, and so it will be, for so it has been, time out
    of mind:
Into the darkness they go, the wise and the lovely.
    Crowned
With lilies and with laurel they go; but I am not resigned.

Lovers and thinkers, into the earth with you.
Be one with the dull, the indiscriminate dust.
A fragment of what you felt, of what you knew,
A formula, a phrase remains, —but the best is lost.

The answer quick and keen, the honest look, the laughter,
    the love, —
They are gone. They have gone to feed the roses. Elegant
    and curled
Is the blossom. Fragrant is the blossom. I know. But I do
    not approve.
More precious was the light in your eyes than all roses in
    the world.

Down, down, down into darkness of the grave
Gently they go, the beautiful, the tender, the kind;
Quietly they go, the intelligent, the witty, the brave.
I know. But I did not approve. And I am not resigned.

Edna St. Vincent
Millay

BUT it doesn't do to be always looking for money. There
was Whaney the miller, he was always wishing to
dream of money like other people. And so he did one night,
that it was hid under the millstone. So before it was hardly
light he went and began to dig and dig, and he never found
the money, but he dug until the mill fell down on himself.   Irish folk tale

I cry to you, but you do not answer me;
you stand off and look at me,
Then you turn upon me without mercy
and with your strong hand you buffet me.
You raise me up and drive me before the wind;
I am tossed about by the tempest.

Indeed I know you will turn me back in death
to the destined place of everyone alive.
Yet should not a hand be held out
to help a wretched man in his calamity?
Or have I not wept for the hardships of others;
was not my soul grieved for the destitute?
Yet when I looked for good, then evil came;
when I expected light, then came darkness.

My soul ebbs away from me;
days of affliction have overtaken me.
My frame takes no rest by night;
my inward parts seethe and will not be stilled.
I go about in gloom, without the sun;

Job 30:20–28   I rise up in public to voice my grief.

E VERY Jew must fulfill all the commandments of the Torah.
And whatever one fails to perform in one incarnation,
must be made up in another. The faults of one incarnation
have to be made good in another because the soul must return
to the throne of glory perfect and without fault. . . .

In his last incarnation this saint had been noted for his
contentment; he was satisfied with little; he was a man who
had not tasted the pleasures of this world—he observed fasts
and devoted himself to study. All his days he had been a man
apart from the vanities of life. When his time came to leave

this world, he experienced very difficult death throes. His body refused to part from his soul and be consigned to a dark grave. His body argued: I have not lived yet, I have not enjoyed my share of life. Every limb resisted the Angel of Death. The heart said: I haven't felt anything yet. The eyes protested: We haven't seen anything yet. The hands: What have we ever held? The legs: Where did we ever go? And so also with all the other parts.   I. L. Peretz

G OD did not make death,
   and does not delight in the death of the living.
For God created all things that they might exist,
and the generative forces of the world are wholesome,
and there is no destructive poison in them;
and the dominion of Hades is not on earth.
For righteousness is immortal.   Wisdom 1:13–15

I can't take in how beautiful this jasmine is. But there is no need to. It is enough simply to believe in miracles in the twentieth century. And I do, even though the lice will be eating me up in Poland before long.   Etty Hillesum

H AD I, out of human weakness,
  hidden my sins
    and buried my guilt in my bosom
Because I feared the noisy multitude
    and the scorn of the tribes terrified me—
    then I should have remained silent,
      and not come out of doors!

Oh, that I had one to hear my case,
    and that my accuser would write
      out his indictment.
Surely, I should wear it on my shoulder
    or put it on me like a diadem;
Of all my steps I should give him an account;
    like a prince I should present
      myself before him.
This is my final plea; let the Almighty
      answer me!

Job 31:33–37

SAM

A RE you suggesting that the Almighty is on the side of the
  killer?

BERISH

He is not on the side of the victim.

SAM

How do you know? Who told you?

BERISH

The killers told me. They told the victims. They always do.
They always say loud and clear that they kill in the name of
God.

SAM

Did the victims tell you? (BERISH *hesitates*) No? Then how do you know? Since when do you take the killers' word for granted? Since when do you place your faith in them? They are efficient killers but poor witnesses.

BERISH

You would like to hear the victims? So would I. But they do not talk. They cannot come to the witness stand. They're dead. You hear me? The witnesses for the prosecution are the dead. All of them. I could call them, summon them a thousand times, and they would not appear here before you. They are not accustomed to taking a walk outside, and surely not on Purim eve. You want to know where they are? At the cemetery. At the bottom of mass graves. I implore the court to consider their absence as the weightiest of proofs, as the heaviest of accusations. They are witnesses, Your Honor, invisible and silent witnesses, but still witnesses! Let their testimony enter your conscience and your memory! Let their premature, unjust deaths turn into an outcry so forceful that it will make the universe tremble with fear and remorse. . . . Take Reb Hayim the scribe, who never squashed a fly or an ant, for they too are God's living creatures; I saw him in agony. I want to know: Who willed his agony? Take Shmuel the cobbler, who treated strangers as though they were his own children; I saw his tears, his last tears. I demand an answer: Who was thirsty for his blood? I want to know: Why was Reb Yiddel the cantor murdered? or Reb Monish his brother? Why were Hava the orphan and her little brother Zisha murdered? So that they could say thank you—and I could say thank you?

SAM

Again you speak for them? You act as though they had appointed you their spokesman. Have they? You knew them—so what? Alive, they were yours; dead, they belong to someone else. The dead belong to the dead, and together they form an immense community reposing in God and loving him the way you have never loved and never will! *(To the court)* He is asking, Why murder—why death? Pertinent questions. But we have some more: Why evil—why ugliness? If God chooses not to answer, he must have his reasons. God is God, and his will is independent from ours—as his reasoning.

MENDEL

What is there left for us to do?

SAM

Endure. Accept. And say Amen.

BERISH

Never! If he wants my life, let him take it. But he has taken other lives—don't tell me they were happy to submit to his will—don't tell me they're happy now! If I'm not, and I'm alive, how can they be? True, they are silent. Good for them and good for him. If they choose to be silent, that's their business! I shall not be!

Elie Wiesel
The Trial of God

L ORD God,
source and destiny of our lives,
in your loving providence
you gave us N.
to grow in wisdom, age, and grace.
Now you have called him/her to yourself.

As we grieve over the loss of one so young,
we seek to understand your purpose.

Draw him/her to yourself
and give him/her full stature in Christ.
May he/she stand with all the angels and saints
who know your love and praise your saving will.

Order of Christian
Funerals

T HOUGH it may be good sometimes to think particularly about God's kindness and worth, and though it may be enlightening too, and a part of contemplation, yet in the work now before us it must be put down and covered with a cloud of forgetting. And you are to step over it resolutely and eagerly, with a devout and kindling love, and try to penetrate that darkness above you. Strike that thick cloud of unknowing with the sharp dart of longing love, and on no account whatever think of giving up.

The Cloud of
Unknowing
Fourteenth century

A HAB told Jezebel all that Elijah had done—that he had put all the prophets to the sword. Jezebel then sent a messenger to Elijah and said, "May the gods do thus and so to me if by this time tomorrow I have not done with your life what was done to each of them." Elijah was afraid and fled for his life, going to Beer-sheba of Judah. He left his servant there and went a day's journey into the desert, until he came to a broom tree and sat beneath it. He prayed for death: "This is enough, O Lord! Take my life, for I am no better than my fathers." He lay down and fell asleep under the broom tree, but then an angel touched him and ordered him to get up and eat. He looked and there at his head was a hearth cake and a jug of water. After he ate and drank, he lay down again, but the angel of the Lord came back a second time, touched him, and ordered, "Get up and eat, else the journey will be too long for you!" He got up, ate and drank; then strengthened by that food, he walked forty days and forty nights to the mountain of God, Horeb.   1 Kings 19:1–8

O NCE I said,
        "In the noontime of life I must depart!
To the gates of the nether world I shall be consigned
    for the rest of my years."
I said, "I shall see the LORD no more
    in the land of the living."
My dwelling, like a shepherd's tent,
    is struck down and borne away from me:
You have folded up my life, like a weaver
    who severs the last thread.
Day and night you give me over to torment:
    I cry out until the dawn.
Like a lion he breaks all my bones;
    [day and night you give me over to torment].
Like a swallow I utter shrill cries;
    I moan like a dove.

My eyes grow weak, gazing heavenward:
O Lord, I am in straits; be my surety!

You have given me health and life;
thus is my bitterness transformed into peace.
You have preserved my life
from the pit of destruction,
When you cast behind your back all my sins.

For it is not the nether world that gives you thanks,
nor death that praises you:
Neither do those who go down into the pit
await your kindness.
The living, the living give you thanks,
as I do today.

Isaiah 38:10–11a,
12–14, 17–19a

S OMETIMES I feel like a motherless child,
Sometimes I feel like a motherless child,
Sometimes I feel like a motherless child,
A long way from home,
A long way from home.

Sometimes I feel like I'm almost gone,
Sometimes I feel like I'm almost gone,
Sometimes I feel like I'm almost gone,
A long way from home,
A long way from home.

Sometimes I feel like a moanin' dove,
Sometimes I feel like a moanin' dove,
Sometimes I feel like a moanin' dove,
A long way from home,
A long way from home.

African-American
spiritual

NABILITY to explain is no ground for disbelief. Not as long as the sense of God persists. I could wish that it did not persist. The contradictions are so painful. No concern for justice? Nothing of pity? Is God only the gossip of the living? Then we watch these living speed like birds over the surface of the water, and one will dive or plunge but not come up again and never be seen any more. And in our turn we will never be seen again, once gone through the surface. We cannot ever say that our knowledge of death is shallow. There is no knowledge. There is longing, suffering, mourning.

Saul Bellow

N facing death, the individual confronts the ultimate humiliation of his or her own demise and the ultimate challenge to affirm the goodness of the whole life, self and cosmos even in the face of death. As psychoanalyst Heinz Kohut puts it, this experience creates the possibility of "a shift of the narcissistic cathexes" (that is, the energy invested in maintaining self-esteem and self-coherence) "to a concept of participation in a supraindividual and timeless existence." Even in a secularized culture, many find themselves at this juncture reaching out for the symbolic expressions that have been sifted and shaped by millenniums of experience within the responsorial rituals of the great religious traditions of humanity.

Mary Frohlich

HIS lyfe, I see, is but a cheyre feyre;
All thingis passen and so most I algate.
To-day I sat full ryall in a cheyere,
Tyll sotell deth knokyd at my gate,
And on-avysed he seyd to me, chek-mate!
Lo! how sotell he maketh a devors—
And worms to fede, he hath here leyd my cors.

Old English verse

I am no longer afraid of death;
I know well
its dark and cold corridors
leading to life.

I am afraid rather of that life
which does not come out of death
which cramps our hands
and retards our march.

I am afraid of my fear
and even more of the fear of others,
who do not know where they are going,
who continue clinging
to what they consider to be life
which we know to be death!

I live each day to kill death;
I die each day to beget life,
and in this dying unto death,
I die a thousand times and
am reborn another thousand
through that love
from my People,

Julia Esquivel   which nourishes hope!

IF a man happens to be 36 years old, as I happen to be,
and some great truth stands before the door of his life,
some great opportunity to stand up for that which is right
and that which is just, and he refuses to stand up because he
wants to live a little longer. . . or he is afraid he will lose his
job. . . he may go on and live until he's 80, and the cessa-
tion of breathing in his life is merely the belated announce-
ment of an earlier death of the spirit.

Man dies when he refuses to stand up for that which is right. A man dies when he refuses to take a stand for that which is true. So we are going to stand up right here . . . letting the world know we are determined to be free.

Martin Luther King, Jr.

D EATH is what takes place within us when we look upon others not as gift, blessing or stimulus but as threat, danger, competition. It is the death that comes to all who try to live by bread alone. This is the death that the Bible fears and gives us good reason to fear. It is not the final departure we think of when we speak of death; it is that purposeless, empty existence devoid of genuine human relationships and filled with anxiety, silence and loneliness.

Dorothy Sölle

F RANZ Jagerstatter was an Austrian peasant beheaded in 1943 for refusing to do any service under Hitler. Franz Jagerstatter's story is so compelling . . . because it is at once such an old story and yet such a modern one. . . . There is one thread in the story that I think is significant for us and for a church in search of models of the gospel life truly lived. The witness for which we honor Franz Jagerstatter was a joint witness; his decision to resist the death was made with Franziska. It was not made without pain or terrible soul-searching for both of them; but it *was* made, with humble clarity of conscience. His was the dramatic action, hers was to live out that act of resistance.

Thomas Gumbleton

I 'M not going to die, honey; I'm going home like a shooting star!

Sojourner Truth
Nineteenth century

d YING is fine)but Death

?o
baby
i

wouldn't like

Death if Death
were
good:for

when(instead of stopping to think)you

begin to feel of it,dying
's miraculous
why?be

cause dying is

perfectly natural; perfectly
putting
it mildly lively(but

Death

is strictly
scientific
& artificial &

evil & legal)

we thank thee
god
almighty for dying

e.e. cummings   (forgive us, o life!the sin of Death

CONVERSION is to see the human face of nuclear war *now*, before it occurs. Conversion means to enter into antici- patory suffering with every potential victim. To see is to act. . . . Conversion always means two things: seeing Jesus and seeing our neighbor. Perhaps when we see Jesus in the faces of the nuclear victims, our hearts will be opened.   Jim Wallis

EVERYTHING leans, like tottering, hunched old women. Every eye shines with fixed waiting
and for the word, "when?"

Here there are few soldiers.
Only the shot-down birds tell of war.

You believe every bit of news you hear.

The buildings now are fuller,
Body smelling close to body,
And the garrets scream with light for long, long hours.

This evening I walked along the street of death.
On one wagon, they were taking the dead away.

Why so many marches have been drummed here?

Why so many soldiers?

Then
A week after the end,
Everything will be empty here.
A hungry dove will peck for bread.
In the middle of the street will stand
An empty, dirty
Hearse.

From a child in a Nazi
concentration camp

THE name of the enemy is death, he said, grinning and shoving his hands in his pockets. Not the death of dying but the living death.

The name of this century is the Century of the Love of Death. Death in this century is not the death people die but the death people live. Men love death because real death is better than living death. That is why men like wars, of course. Bad as wars are and maybe because they are so bad, thinking of peace during war is better than peace. War is what makes peace desirable. But peace without war is intolerable. Why do men settle so easily for lives which are living deaths? Men either kill each other in war, or in peace walk as docilely into living death as sheep into a slaughterhouse.

Walker Percy

I shall die, but that is all that I shall do for Death.
I hear him leading his horse out of the stall; I hear the
    clatter on the barn-floor.
He is in haste; he has business in Cuba, business in the
    Balkans, many calls to make this morning.
But I will not hold the bridle while he cinches the girth.
And he may mount up himself: I will not give him a leg up.

Though he flick my shoulders with his whip, I will not tell
    him which way the fox ran.
With his hoof on my breast, I will not tell him where the
    black boy hides in the swamp.
I shall die, but that is all that I shall do for Death; I am not on
    his pay-roll.

I will not tell him the whereabouts of my friends nor of my
    enemies either.
Though he promise me much, I will not map him the route to
    any man's door.
Am I a spy in the land of the living, that I should deliver men
    to Death?
Brother, the password and the plans of our city are safe with
    me; never through me

Edna St. Vincent
Millay

Shall you be overcome.

THE Lord is my shepherd;
   there is nothing I shall want.
Fresh and green are the pastures
where he gives me repose.
Near restful waters he leads me,
to revive my drooping spirit.

He guides me along the right path;
he is true to his name.
If I should walk in the valley of darkness
no evil would I fear.
You are there with your crook and your staff;
with these you give me comfort.

You have prepared a banquet for me
in the sight of my foes.
My head you have anointed with oil;
my cup is overflowing.

Surely goodness and kindness shall follow me
all the days of my life.
In the Lord's own house shall I dwell
for ever and ever.   Psalm 23

I am the good shepherd. A good shepherd lays down his life
  for the sheep. A hired man, who is not a shepherd and
whose sheep are not his own, sees a wolf coming and leaves
the sheep and runs away, and the wolf catches and scatters
them. This is because he works for pay and has no concern
for the sheep. I am the good shepherd, and I know mine and
mine know me.   John 10:11–14

Hᴏᴡ long, O Lᴏʀᴅ? Will you utterly forget me?
How long will you hide your face from me?
How long shall I harbor sorrow in my soul,
    grief in my heart day after day?
How long will my enemy triumph over me?
Look, answer me, O Lᴏʀᴅ, my God!

Psalm 13:2–4

Hᴏᴘᴇ is, in its most general terms, a sense of the
possible, that what we really need is possible, though
difficult, while hopelessness means to be ruled by a sense of
the impossible. . . . What I hope for I do not yet have or see;
it may be difficult; but I *can* have it—it is possible. Without
this way of feeling about ourselves and things, we do
nothing. We do not act or function. There is no energy
because there is no wishing. And there is no wishing
because there is no sense of the possible.

William F. Lynch

Cʀᴇᴀᴛᴏʀ of the world, keep me sane,
Keep my sense and wisdom, until
You come for me.

Scottish Gaelic song

Sᴇᴇ how the farmer waits for the precious fruit of the earth,
being patient with it until it receives the early and the late
rains. You too must be patient. Make your hearts firm,
because the coming of the Lord is at hand. Do not com-
plain . . . about one another, that you may not be judged.
Behold, the Judge is standing before the gates. Take as an
example of hardship and patience . . . the prophets who
spoke in the name of the Lord. Indeed we call blessed those
who have persevered. You have heard of the perseverance of
Job, and you have seen the purpose of the Lord, because the
Lord is compassionate and merciful.

James 5:7–11

WHEN the Man of Heaven comes in his glory, and all the angels with him, then he will sit on his glorious throne. Before him will be gathered all the nations, and he will separate them one from another as a shepherd separates the sheep from the goats, and he will place the sheep at his right hand, but the goats at the left. Then the king will say to those at his right hand, "Come, O blessed of my Father, inherit the realm prepared for you from the foundation of the world; for I was hungry and you gave me food, I was thirsty and you gave me drink, I was a stranger and you welcomed me, I was naked and you clothed me, I was sick and you visited me, I was in prison and you came to me." Then the righteous will answer him, "Lord, when did we see you hungry and feed you, or thirsty and give you drink? And when did we see you a stranger and welcome you, or naked and clothe you? And when did we see you sick or in prison and visit you?" And the king will answer them, "Truly, I say to you, as you did to one of the littlest of these my dear people, you did it to me."

Matthew 25:31–40

I N waiting we are all alike
in the mind identical
in the art-work of waiting

the nurses' starched caps exclaim
a universe of small perfections
no rituals work here, only mechanics
where returning from the dead
is on schedule, or behind schedule
"in a short while" . . .

Joyce Carol Oates

DEAREST Lord, may I see you today and every day in the
person of your sick, and whilst nursing them minister
unto you. Though you hide yourself behind the unattractive
disguise of the irritable, the exacting, the unreasonable, may
I still recognize you and say: "Jesus, my patient, how sweet it
is to serve you." Lord, give me this seeing faith, then my
work will never be monotonous. I will ever find joy in
humouring the fancies and gratifying the wishes of all poor
sufferers.

O beloved sick, how doubly dear you are to me, when you
personify Christ; and what a privilege is mine to be allowed
to tend you.

Sweetest Lord, make me appreciative of the dignity of my
high vocation, and its many responsibilities. Never permit
me to disgrace it by giving way to coldness, unkindness, or
impatience. And . . . . while you are Jesus, my patient,
deign also to be to me a patient Jesus, bearing with my faults,
looking only to my intention, which is to love and serve you
in the person of each of your sick. Lord, increase my faith,
bless my efforts and work, now and for evermore.

Mother Teresa
of Calcutta

W EAKER and weaker, the sunlight falls
   In the afternoon. The proud and the strong
Have departed.

Those that are left are the unaccomplished.
The finally human.
Natives of a dwindled sphere.

Their indigence is an indigence
That is an indigence of the light,
A stellar pallor that hangs on the threads. . . .

Each person completely touches us
With what he is and as he is,
In the stale grandeur of annihilation.

Wallace Stevens

W ITH beauty before me may I walk,
   With beauty behind me may I walk,
With beauty above me may I walk,
With beauty all around me may I walk.
In old age wandering on a trail of beauty,
Lively, may I walk;
In old age wandering on a trail of beauty,
living again, may I walk.
It is finished in beauty.

Navajo prayer

C ONTINUED life means expectation. Death is the aboli-
  tion of choice. The more choice is limited, the closer
we are to death. The greatest cruelty is to curtail expectations without taking away life completely. A life term in
prison is like that. So is citizenship in some countries. The
best solution would be to live as if the ordinary expectations
had not been removed, not from day to day, blindly. But that
requires immense self-mastery.

Saul Bellow

I N you, O LORD, I take refuge;
     let me never be put to shame.
In your justice rescue me,
     incline your ear to me,
     make haste to deliver me!
Be my rock of refuge,
     a stronghold to give me safety.
You are my rock and my fortress;
     for your name's sake you will lead and guide me.
You will free me from the snare they set for me,
     for you are my refuge.
Into your hands I commend my spirit;
     you will redeem me, O LORD, O faithful God.
You hate those who worship vain idols,
     but my trust is in the LORD.
I will rejoice and be glad of your kindness,
     when you have seen my affliction
     and watched over me in my distress,
Not shutting me up in the grip of the enemy
     but enabling me to move about at large.

Have pity on me, O LORD, for I am in distress;
     with sorrow my eye is consumed; my soul also,
          and my body.
For my life is spent with grief
     and my years with sighing;
My strength has failed through affliction,
     and my bones are consumed.
For all my foes I am an object of reproach
     a laughingstock to my neighbors, and a dread
          to my friends;
     they who see me abroad flee from me.
I am forgotten like the unremembered dead;
     I am like a dish that is broken.
I hear the whispers of the crowd, that frighten me

from every side,
as they consult together against me, plotting
to take my life.
But my trust is in you, O LORD;
I say, "You are my God."
In your hands is my destiny; rescue me
from the clutches of my enemies and my persecutors.
Let your face shine upon your servant;
save me in your kindness.

Psalm 31: 2–17

TARRIE thou with me, O Lord,
for it is toward evening with me,
and the day is far spent,
of this my toilsom life.

Lancelot Andrewes
Seventeenth century

IT is in the small things we see it.
The child's first step,
as awesome as an earthquake.
The first time you rode a bike,
wallowing up the sidewalk.
The first spanking when your heart
went on a journey all alone.
When they called you crybaby
or poor or fatty or crazy
and made you into an alien,
you drank their acid
and concealed it.

Later,
if you faced the death of bombs and bullets
you did not do it with a banner,
you did it with only a hat to
cover your heart.

You did not fondle the weakness inside you
though it was there.
Your courage was a small coal
that you kept swallowing.
If your buddy saved you
and died himself in so doing,
then his courage was not courage,
it was love; love as simple as shaving soap.

Later,
if you have endured a great despair,
then you did it alone,
getting a transfusion from the fire,
picking the scabs off your heart,
then wringing it out like a sock.
Next, my kinsman, you powdered your sorrow,
you gave it a back rub
and then you covered it with a blanket
and after it had slept a while
it woke to the wings of the roses
and was transformed.

Later,
when you face old age and its natural conclusion
your courage will still be shown in the little ways,
each spring will be a sword you'll sharpen,
those you love will live in a fever of love,
and you'll bargain with the calendar
and at the last moment
when death opens the back door
you'll put on your carpet slippers
Anne Sexton   and stride out.

I know no statement of the pathos of the aging spirit more rich and true than the opening lines of William Shakespeare's Sonnet 73. The common image out of which these lines distill their beauty and velocity is the image of a springtime green tree alive with the voices of birds, and that same tree against a sullen, autumnal sky when October shall have come again.

> That time of year thou mayst in me behold
> When yellow leaves, or none, or few, do hang
> Upon those boughs which shake against the cold,
> Bare ruin'd choirs where late the sweet birds sang.

These lines are not the statement of a problem awaiting solution; they are, rather, a statement of the human condition for which there is no solution. The demand is, rather, for courage, acquiescence, resignation, acceptance—some coming to terms with. They are a time of remembering, gathering up and sorting out, discriminating between the abiding and the evanescent, a time of perhaps unmarked passage from knowledge to wisdom, from simple awareness to insight, to what Jonathan Edwards called "consent to being," to the psalmist's "so teach us to number our days that we may get a heart of wisdom," a movement of the total spirit from an anxious hanging-on to a graceful letting-be, a releasement.   Joseph Sittler

I am not eager, bold
Or strong—all that is past.
I am ready *not* to do,   Peter Canisius
At last, at last!   Sixteenth century

THESE are the ones who have survived the time of great distress; they have washed their robes and made them white in the blood of the Lamb.

For this reason they stand before God's throne
    and worship him day and night in his temple.
The one who sits on the throne will shelter them.
They will not hunger or thirst anymore,
    nor will the sun or any heat strike them.
For the Lamb who is in the center of the throne will
      shepherd them
    and lead them to springs of life-giving water,

Revelation 7:14–17   and God will wipe away every tear from their eyes.

To use fresh images confidently Thérèse had first to purge herself of some images of the world to which she was born which had lost their power in her day; some conveyed more superstition than true mystery. The *Grimms' Fairy Tales* of French children were the *Fables of La Fontaine*. In Pauline Martin's copy which Thérèse read as a child, a famous illustration by de Staël pictured Death as a skeleton in a feathered hat. According to Céline, Thérese was "not able to endure this image." During Thérèse's final summer when Pauline was frightened by her coming death Thérèse told her, "It's not 'death' that will come in search of me, it's God."

Patricia O'Connor

We seem to give them back to thee, O God, who gavest them to us. Yet as thou didst not lose them in giving, so do we not lose them by their return. Not as the world giveth, givest thou, O Lover of souls. What thou givest, thou takest not away, for what is thine is ours also if we are thine. And life is eternal and love is immortal, and death is only a horizon, and a horizon is nothing, save the limit of our sight. Lift us up, strong Son of God, that we may see further; cleanse our eyes that we may see more clearly; draw us closer to thyself that we may know ourselves to be nearer to our loved ones who are with thee. And while thou dost prepare a place for us, prepare us also for that happy place, that where thou are we may be also for evermore.

Attributed to
Bede Jarrett

Great Spirit, Great Spirit, my Grandfather, all over the earth the faces of living things are all alike. With tenderness have these come up out of the ground. Look upon these faces of children without number and with children in their arms, that they may face the winds and walk the good road to the day of quiet.

Black Elk

A NNIE folded her arms tightly across her stomach and went outside, and her mother followed.

"How can my grandmother know she will go to Mother Earth when the rug is taken from the loom?" Annie asked.

"Many of the Old Ones know," her mother said.

"How do they know?"

"Your grandmother is one of those who live in harmony with all nature—with earth, coyote, birds in the sky. They know more than many will ever learn. Those Old Ones know." Her mother sighed deeply. "We will speak of other things."

When they reached the small mesa, the Old One sat crossing her knees, folding her gnarled fingers into her lap.

Annie knelt beside her.

The Old One looked far off toward the rim of desert where sky met sand.

"My granddaughter," she said, "you have tried to hold back time. This cannot be done." The desert stretched yellow and brown away to the edge of the morning sky. "The sun comes up from the edge of earth in the morning. It returns to the edge of earth in the evening. Earth, from which good things come for the living creatures on it. Earth, to which all creatures finally go."

Annie picked up a handful of brown sand and pressed it against the palm of her hand. Slowly, she let it fall to earth. She understood many things.

The sun rose but it also set.

The cactus did not bloom forever. Petals dried and fell to earth.

She knew that she was a part of the earth and the things on it. She would always be a part of the earth, just as her grandmother had always been, just as her grandmother would always be, always and forever.

Miska Miles   And Annie was breathless with the wonder of it.

So Janie began to think of Death. Death, that strange being with the huge square toes who lived way in the West. The great one who lived in the straight house like a platform without sides to it, and without a roof. What need has Death for a cover, and what winds can blow against him? He stands in his high house that overlooks the world. Stands watchful and motionless all day with his sword drawn back, waiting for the messenger to bid him come. Been standing there before there was a where or a when or a then. She was liable to find a feather from his wings lying in her yard any day now. She was sad and afraid too.   Zora Neale Hurston

FREE at last, free at last,
I thank God I'm free at last;
Free at last, Free at last,
I thank God I'm free at last.

'Way down yonder in the graveyard walk,
I thank God I'm free at last,
Me and my Jesus goin' to meet and talk,
I thank God I'm free at last.

On my knees when the light passed by,
I thank God I'm free at last,
Thought my soul would rise and fly,
I thank God I'm free at last.

Some of these mornings, bright and fair,
I thank God I'm free at last,
Goin' meet King Jesus in the air,
I thank God I'm free at last.

African-American spiritual

DEAR Don Gustavo, we have to take things as they are. I've had a long life and served the church and left some sort of mark on history. By God's grace I haven't behaved badly: so, not a day more. If the Lord wants me to remain a little longer, well and good, otherwise—we're off.

Pope John XXIII

F OR my part, I'm not aware of having offended anyone, but if I have, I beg their forgiveness; and if you know anyone who has not been edified by my attitudes or actions, ask them to have compassion on me and to forgive me. In this last hour I feel calm and sure that my Lord, in his mercy, will not reject me. Unworthy though I am, I wanted to serve him, and I've done my best to pay homage to truth, justice, charity, and the *cor mitis et humilis* [the meek and humble heart] of the gospel.

Pope John XXIII

H OW happy I shall be if I can still be helpful to you in my grave—so be it. With joy I hasten to meet death. If it comes before I have had the chance to develop all my artistic capacities, it will still be coming too soon despite my harsh fate, and I should probably wish it later—yet even so I should be happy, for would it not free me from a state of endless suffering? Come when thou wilt, I shall meet thee bravely. Farewell and do not wholly forget me when I am dead; I deserve this from you, for during my lifetime I was thinking of you often and of ways to make you happy—please be so.

A letter to his brothers,
Ludwig van Beethoven
Eighteenth century

S HE hadn't any of the sentimentality that comes from a fear of dying. She talked about death as she spoke of a hard winter or a rainy March, or any of the sadnesses of nature.

Willa Cather

WHAT will you have when you finally have me?
Nothing.
Nothing I have not already given
freely each day I spent
not waiting for you
but living
as if the shifting shadows of grapes
and fine-pointed leaves in the shelter
of the arbor would continue to tremble
when my eyes were absent
in memory of my seeing,
or the books fall open where I marked them
when my astonishment overflowed
at a gift come unsummoned, this love
for the open hands of poems,
earth fruit, sun soured grass, the steady
outward lapping stillness of midnight
snowfalls, an arrow of light waking me
on certain mornings with sharp wound
so secret that not even you
will have it when you have me.
You will have my fingers
but not what they touched. Some gestures
outflowing from a rooted being, the memory
of morning light cast on a bed
where two lay together—
the shining curve of flesh!—
they will forever be out of your reach
whose care is with the husks.

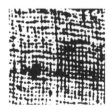

Michele Murray

IN order to possess what you do not possess
You must go by the way of dispossession   T. S. Eliot

WHAT the world could be
is my good dream . . .
I think of a luxury
in the sturdiness and grace
of necessary things, not
in frivolity. That would heal
the earth, and heal men.
But the end, too, is part
of the pattern, the last
labor of the heart:
to learn to lie still,
one with the earth
Wendell Berry   again, and let the world go.

THE grave seemed narrow to me, too narrow for so huge a
number of men and women. The earth is deceptive.
Alive, man needs room: offices, palaces, workshops, stores;
dead, he needs but his own space: a tiny crack on the earth's
Elie Wiesel   surface.

AND when from death I'm free,
I'll sing on, I'll sing on.
And when from death I'm free,
I'll sing and joyful be,
And through eternity,
I'll sing on, I'll sing on,
And through eternity,
Southern folk hymn   I'll sing on.

EVERYMAN

F ULL unready I am such reckoning to give.
I know thee not. What messenger art thou?

DEATH

I am Death, that no man dreadeth,
For every man I rest, and no man spareth;
For it is God's commandment
That all to me should be obedient.

EVERYMAN

O Death, thou comest when I had thee least in mind!
In thy power it lieth me to save;
Yet of my good will I give thee, if thou will be kind—
Yea, a thousand pound shalt thou have—
And defer this matter till another day.

DEATH

Everyman, it may not be, by no way.
I set not by gold, silver, nor riches,
Ne by pope, emperor, king, duke, ne princes;
For, and I would receive gifts great,
All the world I might get;
But my custom is clean contrary.   *Everyman*
I give thee no respite. Come hence, and not tarry.   Sixteenth century

I N the Nuremburg war-crime trials a witness appeared who
had lived for a time in a grave in a Jewish graveyard, in
Vilna, Poland. It was the only place he—and many others—
could live, when in hiding after they had escaped the gas
chamber. During this time he wrote poetry, and one of the
poems was a description of birth. In a grave nearby a young
woman gave birth to a boy. The 80-year-old gravedigger,

wrapped in a linen shroud, assisted. When the newborn child uttered his first cry, the old man prayed: "Great God, hast thou finally sent the Messiah to us? For who else than the Messiah himself can be born in a grave?" But after three days the poet saw the child sucking his mother's tears because she had no milk for him.

This story, which surpasses anything the human imagination could have invented, has not only incomparable emotional value, but also tremendous symbolic power. When I first read it, it occurred to me more forcefully than ever before that our Christian symbols, taken from the gospel stories, have lost a great deal of their power because they are too often repeated and too superficially used. It has been forgotten that the manger of Christmas was the expression of utter poverty and distress before it became the place where the angels appeared and to which the star pointed. And it has been forgotten that the tomb of Jesus was the end of his life and of his work *before* it became the place of his final triumph. We have become insensitive to the infinite tension which is implied in the words of the Apostles' Creed: "suffered . . . was crucified, dead, and buried . . . rose again from the dead." We already know, when we hear the first words, what the ending will be: "rose again"; and for many people it is no more than the inevitable "happy ending." The old Jewish gravedigger knew better. For him, the immeasurable tension implicit in the expectation of the Messiah was a reality, appearing in the infinite contrast between the things he saw and the hope he maintained.

The depth of this tension is emphasized by the last part of the story. After three days the child was not elevated to glory; he drank his mother's tears, having nothing else to drink. Probably he died and the hope of the old Jew was frustrated once more, as it had been frustrated innumerable times before. No consolation can be derived from this story; there cannot be a happy ending—and precisely this is the truth about our lives. In a remarkable passage of his book, *Credo*, Karl Barth writes about the word "buried" in the Creed: "By a man's being buried it is evidently confirmed and sealed— seemingly in his presence, actually already in his absence—

that he *has* no longer a present, any more than a future. He has become pure past. He is accessible only to memory, and even that only so long as those who are able and willing to remember him are not themselves buried. And the future toward which all human present is running is just this: to be buried." These words describe exactly the situation in which the pious old Jew prayed: "Great God, hast thou finally sent the Messiah to us?"

We often hide the seriousness of the "buried" in the Creed, not only for the Christ, but also for ourselves, by imagining that not *we* shall be buried, but only a comparatively unimportant part of us, the physical body. That is not what the Creed implies. It is the same subject, Jesus Christ, of whom it is said that he suffered and that he was buried and that he was resurrected. *He* was buried, he—his *whole* personality—was removed from the earth. The same is true of us. *We* shall die, we—our *personality*, from which we cannot separate our body as an accidental part—shall be buried.

Only if we take the "buried" in the gospel stories as seriously as this, can we evaluate the Easter stories and can we evaluate the words of the gravedigger, "Who else than the Messiah can be born in a grave?" His question has two aspects. Only the Messiah can bring birth out of death. It is not a natural event. It does not happen every day, but it happens on the day of the Messiah. It is the most surprising, the most profound, and the most paradoxical mystery of existence. Arguments for the immortality of an assumedly better part of us cannot bring life out of the grave. Eternal life is brought about only with the coming of the "new reality," the eon of the Messiah, which, according to *our* faith, has already appeared in Jesus as the Christ.

But there is another side to the assertion that nobody other than the Messiah can be born in a grave, a side which, perhaps, was less conscious to the pious Jew. The Christ *must* be buried in order to be the "Christ," namely, he who has conquered death. The gospel story we have heard assures us of the real and irrevocable death and burial of Jesus. The women, the high priests, the soldiers, the sealed stone—they are all called by the gospel to witness the reality of the end. We ought to listen more carefully to these witnesses, to the ones who tell us with triumph or cynicism that he has been buried, that he is removed forever from the earth, that no real traces of him are left in our world. And we ought also to listen to the others who say, in doubt and despair, "But we trusted that it had been he who should have redeemed Israel." It is not hard to hear both these voices today, in a world where there are so many places like the Jewish cemetery in Vilna. It is even possible to hear them in ourselves, for each of us to hear them in ourselves.

And, if we hear them, what can we answer? Let us be clear about this. The answer of Easter is not a necessity. In reality, there is no inevitable happy ending as there is in perverted and perverting cinemas. But the answer of Easter has become possible precisely because the Christ has been buried. The new life would not really be *new* life if it did not come from the complete end of the old life. Otherwise, it would have to be buried again. But if the new life has come out of the grave, then the Messiah himself has appeared.

Paul Tillich

G LORY, glory, hallelujah,
   When I lay my burden down.
I'll be leaving all my troubles
     When I lay my burden down.
I'll be crossing over Jordan
     When I lay my burden down.
I'll be marching in the kingdom
     When I lay my burden down.
I'll be climbing Jacob's ladder
     When I lay my burden down.
I'll be resting from my labors
     When I lay my burden down.
Glory, glory, hallelujah,
     When I lay my burden down.

African-American
spiritual

THE divine countenance
is capable of maddening and driving
all souls out of their senses
with longing for it.
When it does this by its very divine nature
it is thereby
drawing all things to itself.
   Every creature
   Every creature—
whether it knows it or not—
seeks repose.

Meister Eckhart
Fourteenth century

THROUGH fields of ripe wheat
In France, in the heart of France
We've come on foot from Paris
To these incredible stones
To this tidal wave of the Sabbath
Rising up out of the wheat
With its portals crowded with prophets
With patriarchs and with martyrs
Tall in the long folds
Of their carven robes.

This one is Abraham
With one hand he's holding the knife
The knife of sacrifice
And with his other hand
He's tenderly cupping the cheek
Of Isaac, his little son
There's a look of calm wonder
On the face of his little son
And under his feet is the ram
The ram who will take his place
As the victim of sacrifice.

Abraham, it's you especially
Whom I have come to see
You are our father in faith
In this knapsack on my back
I'm bringing you all the deaths
That I can't understand
And not the deaths alone
But also the pain
The deaths from all the famines
From holocaust and war
And every unjust death
Of the innocent and the humble.

To take the place of the child
Isaac there was a ram
But for all of those others
There was no ram
   And I lay down all these deaths
I lay them down at your feet
So that you can keep them for me
Since by myself
I am unable
To understand them.

Anne Porter

A ND so was he brought by Mr. Lieutenant out of the Tower, and from thence led toward the place of execution, where going up the scaffold, which was so weak that it was ready to fall, he said to Mr. Lieutenant, "I pray you, I pray you, Mr. Lieutenant, see me safe up, and for my coming down let me shift for myself." Then desired he all the people thereabouts to pray for him, and to bear witness with him, that he should then suffer death in and for the faith of the holy Catholic church, which done he kneeled down, and after his prayers said, he turned to the executioner, and with a cheerful countenance spake unto him. "Pluck up thy spirits, man, and be not afraid to do thine office, my neck is very short. Take heed therefore thou shoot not awry for saving thine honesty." So passed Sir Thomas More out of this world to God upon the very same day in which himself had most desired.

William Roper
Sixteenth century

ALL of us, I think, participate to some degree in the "psychic numbing" required to be an effective missileer. The Yale University psychiatrist Robert Jay Lifton coined this term to describe the process of deadening our awareness and feelings to the real possibility of a nuclear war. This numbing of awareness allows us to effectively build, maintain, refine and deploy ever-increasing destructive weapons with an unquestioned sense of righteousness and purpose, all in the name of the national defense. We are all leading double lives, according to Lifton: aware on the one hand of the threat of complete nuclear annihilation and extinction of our species, and on the other hand, behaving as if no such threat existed. Lifton says that the extent to which most of us block out conscious thought of the implications of the nuclear arms race is neurotic, and downright dangerous.

Jay Bayerl
Takoma Park City
Newsletter

THE world's an orphan's home. Shall
we never have peace without sorrow?
without pleas of the dying for
help that won't come? O
quiet form upon the dust, I cannot
look and yet I must. If these great patient
dyings—all these agonies
and woundbearings and bloodshed—
can teach us how to live, these
dyings were not wasted.

Marianne Moore

O the night of the weeping children!
 O the night of the children branded for death!
Sleep may not enter here.
Terrible nursemaids
Have usurped the place of mothers,
Have tautened their tendons with the false death,
Sow it on to the walls and into the beams—
Everywhere it is hatched in the nests of horror.
Instead of mother's milk, panic suckles those little ones.

Yesterday Mother still drew
Sleep toward them like a white moon,
There was the doll with cheeks derouged by kisses
In one arm,
The stuffed pet, already
Brought to life by love,
In the other—
Now blows the wind of dying,
Blows the shifts over the hair
That no one will comb again.   Nelly Sachs

ALTHOUGH in imagination we can try to survey the whole
prospective scene of destruction, inquiring into how
many would live and how many would die and how far the
collapse of the environment would go under attacks of
different sizes, and piling up statistics on how many square
miles would be lethally contaminated, or what percentage
of the population would receive first-, second-, or third-
degree burns, or be trapped in the rubble of its burning
houses, or be irradiated to death, no one actually experienc-
ing a holocaust would have any such overview. The news of
other parts necessary to put together that picture would be
one of the things that were immediately lost, and each
surviving person, with vision drastically foreshortened by
the collapse of this world, and impressions clouded by pain,

shock, bewilderment, and grief, would see only as far as whatever scene of chaos and agony happened to lie at hand. For it would not be only such abstractions as "industry" and "society" and "the environment" that would be destroyed in a nuclear holocaust; it would also be, over and over again, the small collections of cherished things, known landscapes, and beloved people that made up the immediate contents of individual lives. . .

To employ a mathematical analogy, we can say that although the risk of extinction may be fractional, the stake is, humanly speaking, infinite, and a fraction of infinity is still infinity. In other words, once we learn that a holocaust *might* lead to extinction we have no right to gamble, because if we lose, the game will be over, and neither we nor anyone else will ever get another chance. Therefore, although, scientifically speaking, there is all the difference in the world between the mere possibility that a holocaust will bring about extinction and the certainty of it, morally they are the same, and we have no choice but to address the issue of nuclear weapons as though we knew for a certainty that their use would put an end to our species. In weighing the fate of the earth and, with it, our own fate, we stand before a mystery, and in tampering with the earth we tamper with a mystery. We are in deep ignorance. Our ignorance should dispose us to wonder, our wonder should make us humble, our humility should inspire us to reverence and caution, and our reverence and caution should lead us to act without delay to withdraw the threat we
Jonathan Schell   now pose to the earth and to ourselves.

I was still thinking of . . . boys I knew for whom there had been no difference between war and peace, who had returned from Vietnam so scarred within and without that they couldn't fit into the society they had been sent to defend, boys wounded more by sights and deeds than bullets. At the top of the hill I sat beneath a sycamore and stared idly across the next valley at the trees and scrub brush on the opposite slope, my thoughts on the folly and inev-
Stephen Greenleaf   itability of war.

A robin redbreast in a cage
Puts all Heaven in a rage.

A dog starv'd at his master's gate
Predicts the ruin of the State.

Each outcry of the hunted hare
A fibre from the brain does tear.

A skylark wounded in the wing,
A cherubim does cease to sing.

The wild deer, wandering here and there.
Keeps the Human soul from care.

He who shall hurt the little wren
Shall never be belov'd by men.

The wanton boy that kills the fly
Shall feel the spider's enmity.

The caterpillar on the leaf
Repeats to thee thy mother's grief.

Kill not the moth or butterfly.
For the Last Judgment draweth nigh.

William Blake
Eighteenth century

I N the sweat of your face
you shall eat bread
till you return to the ground,
    for out of it you were taken;
you are dust,

Genesis 3:19   and to dust you shall return.

T HE beautiful pine casket in which Dorothy Day's body
lay during the 1980 wake at Maryhouse, the funeral at
Nativity Church around the corner and burial on Staten
Island was so strikingly apt that it shocked one into con-
sciousness of the incongruity of most coffins. It served so
aptly the plain simplicity, grace, discernment, insight, honesty, directness, dignity of that great woman's remarkable
life and ministry. The body was the sign, not the casket, and
yet the casket communicated a craft and showed a care
befitting its servant role.

Robert W. Hovda

D EAR friends, at the very beginning of our scriptures we
read that God looked each day at creation and saw
how good it was. The very dust is good in God's eyes. From it
we come and to it we return. What is to come is in the hands
of our God who rejoiced to create us. We leave here (to the
earth, to the waters, to the wind) these ashes, but we carry
within us the memory of N. and the praise of our God who is
manifest and blessed in every life.

Let us pray.

Our days, O Lord, are like those of grass.
Like a flower of the field we bloom.
The wind sweeps over us and we are gone
and our place knows us no more.
But your kindness is from eternity
and to eternity,

your justice is new in every generation.
Receive our brother/sister N.
Do not deal with him/her according to his/her sins
but crown him/her instead with your kindness.
Like a father and a mother, shelter and embrace him/her.
For N.'s life among us we give you thanks
and we ask to praise you with him/her
for ever and ever.   Gabe Huck

THE words of the first and the last, who died and came to
life: "Be faithful unto death, and I will give you the
crown of life."   Revelation 2:8, 10

THE use of crowns of foliage in the rites of the feast of
Tabernacles is attested both by Jewish documents about
the feast and by Judeo-Christian documents which show it
persisting in the rites of baptism. This enables us to arrive at
one last aspect of the Jewish symbolism of the feast. The
eschatological character of the crown as denoting eternal
blessedness is clear. . . . There is a whole series of Jewish
and Christian texts in which the crown is the symbol of the   Jean Daniélou
glory of the elect, in the biblical sense of the word, and of the   *Primitive Christian*
imperishable life which is their lot.   *Symbols*

FOR I am already being poured out like a libation, and the
time of my departure is at hand. I have competed well; I
have finished the race; I have kept the faith. From now on the
crown of righteousness awaits me, which the Lord, the just
judge, will award to me on that day, and not only to me, but
to all who have longed for his appearance.   2 Timothy 4:6–8

O Almighty God, the God of the spirits of all flesh, who by a voice from heaven didst proclaim, Blessed are the dead who die in the Lord: Multiply, we beseech thee, to those who rest in Jesus the manifold blessings of thy love, that the good work which thou didst begin in them may be made perfect unto the day of Jesus Christ. And of thy mercy, O heavenly Father, grant that we, who now serve thee on earth, may at last, together with them, be partakers of the inheritance of the saints in light; for the sake of thy Son Jesus Christ our Lord.

Book of Common Prayer

So we do not lose heart. Though our outer nature is wasting away, our inner nature is being renewed every day. For this slight momentary affliction is preparing for us an eternal weight of glory beyond all comparison, because we look not to the things that are seen but to the things that are unseen; for the things that are seen are transient, but the things that are unseen are eternal.

For we know that if the earthly tent we live in is destroyed, we have a building from God, a house not made with hands, eternal in the heavens.

2 Corinthians 4:16—5:1

BECAUSE I could not stop for Death,
He kindly stopped for me;
The carriage held but just ourselves
And Immortality.

We slowly drove, he knew no haste,
And I had put away
My labor, and my leisure too,
For his civility.

We passed the school where children played
At wrestling in the ring;
We passed the fields of grazing grain,
We passed the setting sun.

We paused before a house that seemed
A swelling of the ground;
The roof was scarcely visible,
The cornice but a mound.

Since then 'tis centuries; but each
Feels shorter than the day
I first surmised the horses' heads
Were toward eternity.

Emily Dickinson
Nineteenth century

Francis of Assisi
Thirteenth century

PRAISED be my Lord for our sister, the death of the body,
from which no one escapes.

LONG ago your servant Francis
praised you, O God, for all your creatures.
For brother sun and sister moon he sang to you,
for wind and water, birds and beasts.
He praised you even for death.
So be praised, my Lord, for Sister Death,
most kind and gentle death
that leads home your son/daughter N.
In suffering he/she learned how this life is an exile,
this world a place of tears.
We give you thanks for the blessing he/she was
        in our midst.
May N. now find rest with all your holy ones,
and with them may he/she sing your praise
        for ever and ever.

Gabe Huck

I learned early to keep death in my line of sight, keep it
under surveillance, keep it on clear guard and away from
any brush where it might coil unnoticed.

Joan Didion

O GOD,
You are water for our thirst,
and manna in our desert.
We praise you for the life of N.
and bless your mercy
that has brought his/her suffering to an end.
Now we beg that same endless mercy
to raise him/her to new life.
Nourished by the food and drink of heaven,
may he/she rest for ever
in the joy of Christ our Lord.

*Order of Christian
Funerals*

COWARDS die many times before their deaths;
The valiant never taste of death but once.
Of all wonders that I yet have heard,
It seems to me most strange that men should fear,   .
Seeing that death, a necessary end,
Will come when it will come.

William Shakespeare
Sixteenth century

IN New Mexico there were an ancient people called the Mimbres. They were skilled potters. What they made was far superior to the work of later potters in the Southwest. The Mimbres formed bowls out of rich, red clay that held generations of life, and they painted that shaped clay with animals, people, plants, and even the dusty wind that still inhabits the dry New Mexico land.

Like the Anasazi and other ancient nations, these were people of the mystery, having abandoned their place and vanished into a dimension that has remained unknown to those of us who have come later. But before they disappeared into the secret, the Mimbres "killed" their pots by breaking a hole in the center of each one. It is thought that the hole served to release the spirit of the pot from the clay, allowing it to travel with them over land and to join them in their burial grounds. It is called a "kill hole." . . .

Sometimes death has such a strange way of turning things inside out, so that what is gone becomes as important as what remains. Such an absence defines our world as surely as a Mimbres pot contains a bowl of air, or as a woman's dying body holds a memory and history of life.

Linda Hogan

BRIDEGROOM and Lord, the longed-for hour has come! It is time for us to see one another, my Beloved, my Master. It is time for me to set out. Let us go.

Teresa of Avila
Sixteenth century

ONE might say that an apparition is human vision corrected by divine love. I do not see you as you really are, Joseph; I see you through my affection for you. The miracles of the church seem to me to rest not so much upon faces or voices or healing power coming suddenly near to us from afar off, but upon our perceptions being made finer, so that for a moment our eyes can see and our ears can hear what is there about us always.

Willa Cather

COME lovely and soothing death,
Undulate round the world, serenely arriving,
    arriving,
In the day, in the night, to all, to each,
Sooner or later delicate death.

Prais'd be the fathomless universe,
For life and joy, and for objects and knowledge curious,
And for love, sweet love—but praise! praise! praise!
For the sure-enwinding arms of cool-enfolding death.

Dark mother always gliding near with soft feet,
Have none chanted for thee a chant of fullest welcome?
Then I chant it for thee, I glorify thee above all,
I bring thee a song that when thou must indeed come,
    come unfalteringly.

Walt Whitman
Nineteenth century

IF I must die,
I will encounter darkness as a bride
And hug it in mine arms.

William Shakespeare
Sixteenth century

L ET nothing trouble you, let nothing frighten you: who-   Teresa of Avila
ever has God lacks nothing. God alone is enough.   Sixteenth century

B LIND Francis, waiting to welcome Sister Death,
Worn though he was by ecstasies and fame,
Had heart for tune. With what remained of breath
He led his friars in canticles.

                    Then came
Brother Elias, scowling, to his side,
Small-souled Elias, crying by book and candle,
This was outrageous! Had the monks no pride?
Music at deathbeds! Ah, the shame, the scandal!

Elias gave him sermons and advice
Instead of song; which simply proves once more
What things are sure this side of paradise:
Death, taxes, and the counsel of the bore.
Though we outwit the tithe, make death our friend,
Bores we have with us even to the end.   Phyllis McGinley

Y OU see the creatures die, and you know you will die.
And one day it occurs to you that you must not need life.
Obviously. And then you're gone. You have finally under-
stood that you're dealing with a maniac.

I think that the dying pray at the last, not "please," but "thank
you," as a guest thanks his host at the door. Falling from
airplanes, the people are crying, "thank you, thank you," all
down the air; and the cold carriages draw up for them on the
rocks. Divinity is not playful. The universe was not made in
jest but in solemn, incomprehensible earnest. By a power
that is unfathomably secret, and holy, and fleet. There is
nothing to be done about it, but ignore it, or see. And then
you walk fearlessly, eating what you must, growing wherever you can, like the monk on the road who knows

precisely how vulnerable he is, who takes no comfort among death-forgetting men, and who carries his vision of vastness and might around in his tunic like a live coal, which neither burns nor warms him, but with which he will not part.

Annie Dillard

S TEAL away, steal away,
Steal away to Jesus!
Steal away, steal away home,
I ain't got long to stay here.

My Lord, he calls me,
He calls me by the thunder;
The trumpet sounds within my soul;
I ain't got long to stay here.

Green trees are bending,
Poor sinners stand a trembling;
The trumpet sounds within my soul;
I ain't got long to stay here.

My Lord, he calls me,
He calls me by the lightning;
The trumpet sounds within my soul;
I ain't got long to stay here.

African-American
spiritual

I T is good to wait in silence for the Lord.

Lamentations 3:26

THERE is, after all, a mysterious—in the sense that it inspires wonder, when we come to think about it— bond connecting us all. Rich or poor, we are, at the heart of it, bone of the same Adam's rib. We share a common subway ride across this orb in time. Our destination is ultimately the same, and as Charles Péguy said, when we get to heaven, God will ask, "Where are the others?"

Commonweal

IF one part suffers, all the parts suffer with it; if one part is honored, all the parts share its joy.

1 Corinthians 12:26

TOUCHING someone is a sign of transferring something of oneself to another. It is one of the most universal of natural signs and hence, perhaps the most apt sacramental sign or gesture. When trying to comfort someone bereaved and all words fail, we touch that person, perhaps place our hands on his or her shoulder as a sign that we deeply care, we share our love. On the part of the person who touches, the gesture often implies gentle affection, protection, or communication of strength. To allow another person to touch me is an act of openness, of acceptance on my part of what that person wishes to communicate or to give me in love.

Godfrey Diekmann

FATHER of compassion,
shelter them under the shadow of your wings for ever
and let their souls be bound in the bundle of life.

Jewish burial rite

THERE were some men and women who, in many places, did opt for humanity. Surrounded by terror, oppressed by absolute evil, they had the courage to care about their fellow human beings. . . . They were alone—as the victims themselves were alone—so the question we must confront is what made them so special, so human, so different?

The principle that governs the biblical vision of society is "Thou shall not stand idly by when another is hurting, suffering, or being victimized." It is because that injunction was ignored or violated that the catastrophe involving such multitudes occurred. The victims perished not only because of the killers, but also because of the apathy of the bystanders.

Elie Wiesel

BUT the additional curse of happy families, I reflected, was to fear the loss of one of its members, to be unmanned by every accident that could befall a child or a husband or a mother. The lives of the happily united were not necessarily tranquil. In fact everything was precarious: Those who live in solitude need only fear their own mortality.

Anita Brookner

I'LL be singing up there,
I'll be singing up there,
Oh! come on up to bright glory,
I'll be singing up there.

If you miss me singing down here,
If you miss me singing down here,
Oh, come on up to bright glory,
You'll find me singing up there.

If you miss me praying down here,
If you miss me praying down here,
Oh, come on up to bright glory,
You'll find me praying up there.

If you miss me walking down here,
If you miss me walking down here,
Oh, come on up to bright glory,
You'll find me walking up there.

If you miss me shouting down here,
If you miss me shouting down here,
Oh, come on up to bright glory,
You'll find me shouting up there.

African-American
spiritual

WE tried to let you know why it was so important to be an honest human being. First, by always being honest with yourself, you cannot help but be honest and honorable to others. Be proud of yourself, not only in who and what you are, but also in what you do to make the world a more decent world for others less fortunate than you. Be compassionate and charitable to them and try to share what you have in a real way with those who can benefit by your caring. Fight for what you believe in, and though your path may not be an easy one, know that your concern adds strength to others who need it as well as adding strength to yourself.

From a will

THOSE who are dead have never gone away.
They are in the shadows darkening around,
They are in the shadows fading into day,
The dead are not under the ground.
They are in the trees that quiver,
They are in the woods that weep,
They are in the waters of the rivers,
They are in the waters that sleep.
They are in the crowds, they are in the homestead.
The dead are never dead.

Birago Diop

A few light taps upon the pane made him turn to the window. It had begun to snow again. He watched sleepily the flakes, silver and dark, falling obliquely against the lamplight. The time had come for him to set out on his journey westward. Yes, the newspapers were right; snow was general all over Ireland. It was falling on every part of the dark central plain, on the treeless hills, falling softly upon the Bog of Allen and, farther westward, softly falling into the dark mutinous Shannon waves. It was falling, too, upon every part of the lonely churchyard on the hill where Michael Furey lay buried. It lay thickly drifted on the crooked crosses and headstones, on the spears of the little gate, on the barren thorns. His soul swooned slowly as he heard the snow falling faintly through the universe and faintly falling, like the descent of their last end, upon all the living and the dead.

James Joyce

U NFORTUNATELY, in our society we keep death hidden. Few people have or seek the opportunity to witness the death of others. They would feel out of place as idle specta- tors. But this is perhaps because we do not have a Christian understanding of death in which the spectator is not idle at all but represents the active support and encouragement of the community. To witness death, however, places the same sort of demands on a person as the receiving of a confession of sin. It demands that one have come to terms rather radically with one's own approaching death as a dimension of life in the present.

Monika Hellwig

T HE worst is done and it has been mended, and all will be well, and all will be well, and all will be very well.

Juliana of Norwich
Fourteenth century

S AINT Joseph, pray for us.
Comfort of the troubled, pray for us.
Hope of the sick, pray for us.
Patron of the dying, pray for us.
Terror of evil spirits, pray for us.

Litany of St. Joseph

M INISTERING to AIDS patients means . . . entering into a world of pain and distress with sympathy and soli- darity. I don't see that the church has a choice whether or not to turn to this group of people, whether or not to care for them, not even if the life-style of this group is considered to be sinful (then the church would not have to care for anybody).

How about my ability to minister to patients with a life- style foreign to my own? How about my ability to come to terms with my own mortality when confronted with the deaths of so many young patients? How about my fear of touching those who are "untouchable and unclean"? How about my hope, my strength, my joy, my faith, when getting involved in human tragedies of that dimension?

Klaus Wendler

Eudora Welty

WHAT burdens we lay on the dying.

WELCOME your servant, Lord, into the place of salvation
which because of your mercy s/he rightly hoped for.
Lord, save your people.
Deliver your servant, Lord, from every distress.
Lord, save your people.
Deliver your servant, Lord, as you delivered Noah
from the flood.
Lord, save your people.
Deliver your servant, Lord, as you delivered Abraham
from Ur of the Chaldees.
Lord, save your people.
Deliver your servant, Lord, as you delivered Job
from his sufferings.
Lord, save your people.
Deliver your servant, Lord, as you delivered Moses
from the hand of the Pharaoh.
Lord, save your people.
Deliver your servant, Lord, as you delivered Daniel
from the den of lions.
Lord, save your people.
Deliver your servant, Lord, as you delivered the three young
men from the fiery furnace.
Lord, save your people.
Deliver your servant, Lord, as you delivered Susanna
from her false accusers.
Lord, save your people.
Deliver your servant, Lord, as you delivered David
from the attacks of Saul and Goliath.
Lord, save your people.
Deliver your servant, Lord, as you delivered Peter and Paul
from prison.
Lord, save your people.

Commendation
of the Dying,
*Pastoral Care
of the Sick*

Deliver your servant, Lord, through Jesus our Savior, who
suffered death for us and gave us eternal life.
Lord, save your people.

D IDN'T my Lord deliver Daniel, deliver Daniel, deliver
Daniel?
Didn't my Lord deliver Daniel?
Then why not everyone?

African-American
spiritual

E VERY breath we breathe is a finite number away from the
last. They are part and parcel, this breath and our last, the
same river that later runs into the sea.

We have been conditioned to see it otherwise. We think, *this*
is life and *that* is death. We love and hate and plan and play as
if there were no tomorrow in which we won't figure—trying
to whistle past that bigger graveyard.

Along came AIDS, death with a different mask, defying us to
look away.

Michael J. Farrell

D E profundis clamavi ad te, Domine,
Domine, exaudi vocem meam.

Out of the depths I cry to you, O LORD;
   LORD, hear my voice!
Let your ears be attentive
   to my voice in supplication:

If you, O LORD, mark iniquities,
   LORD, who can stand?
But with you is forgiveness,
   that you may be revered.

I trust in the LORD;
   my soul trusts in his word.
My soul waits for the LORD
   more than sentinels wait for the dawn.

More than sentinels wait for the dawn,
   let Israel wait for the LORD,

For with the LORD is kindness
  and with him is plenteous redemption;
And he will redeem Israel
Psalm 130   from all their iniquities.

H ERE is a man suffering on his bed of pain, and the
church comes to him to perform the sacrament of
healing. For this man, as for every person and the whole
world, suffering can be *the* defeat, the way of a complete
surrender to darkness, despair and solitude. It can be *dying*
in the very real sense of the word. And yet it can be also the
ultimate victory of a person and of Life in that person. The
church does not come to restore *health* in this man, simply
to replace medicine when medicine has exhausted its own
possibilities. The church comes to take this man into the
Love, the Light and the Life of Christ. It comes not merely to
"comfort" him in his sufferings, not to "help" him, but to
make him a *martyr,* a *witness* to Christ in his very sufferings.
A martyr is one who beholds "the heavens opened, and the
Son of Man standing on the right hand of God" (Acts 7:56). A
martyr is one for whom God is not another—and the last—
chance to stop the awful pain; God is his very life, and thus
Alexander   everything in his life comes to God, ascends to the fullness of
Schmemann   Love.

F INDING this cavern—
following the lantern light . . .
Haiku   followed by silence.

JESUS' awareness of his impending death permeates his actions and can be compared, I believe, to the knowledge held today by the terminally ill.

Those who rely on the motto "Make every day count" also know that continuous preoccupation with their own illness and death is not the way to accomplish their aim. There is a necessary setting aside of focus on one's death, not a "denial" but an attempt to gain the energy for involvement with what every day brings. Within the world of the terminally ill, then, a time to rejoice is not a rejection of the reality of illness. It is instead at minimum a necessary coping strategy. Jesus on Palm Sunday may be likened to the cancer patient who celebrates an anniversary—fully aware of the "lastness" of it all, yet celebrating nonetheless.

Lucy Bregman

RIDE on, ride on in majesty
In lowly pomp ride on to die.
O Christ, your triumphs now begin
O'er captive death and conquered sin.

Henry H. Milman
Nineteenth century

BLESSED are you, Lord, God of all creation,
the true Judge.

Jewish prayer on
hearing of or
witnessing a death

GO forth, Christian soul, from this world
in the name of God the almighty Father,
who created you,
in the name of Jesus Christ, Son of the
living God,
who suffered for you,
in the name of the Holy Spirit,
who was poured out upon you,
go forth, faithful Christian.

*Pastoral Care
of the Sick*

IT is the will of him who sent me that I should lose nothing of what he has given me: rather, that I should raise it up on the last day." (John 6:39) That is our faith conviction about life in Christ. But we need to know what we do. We counter the mystery of death with a greater mystery still, the mystery of risen life. In the meantime there is grief, and nothing in Christian faith asks us to deny grief. We have known, all of us, someone who made an immense difference. We thank God for just that much. And we ask God for just enough strength to handle our grief.

Gerard S. Sloyan

NOTHING can make up for the absence of someone whom we love, and it would be wrong to try to find a substitute; we must simply hold out and see it through. That sounds very hard at first, but at the same time it is a great consolation, for the gap, as long as it remains unfilled, preserves the bonds between us. It is nonsense to say that God fills the gap; God doesn't fill it, but on the contrary, keeps it empty and so helps us to keep alive our former communion with each other, even at the cost of pain.

Dietrich Bonhoeffer

Edna St. Vincent Millay

THE presence of that absence is everywhere.

WE, the rescued,
    Beg you:
Show us your sun, but gradually.
Lead us from star to star, step by step.
Be gentle when you teach us to live again.
Lest the song of a bird,
Or the pail being filled at the well,
Let our badly sealed pain burst forth again.

Nelly Sachs

G OD of all consolation,
in your unending love and mercy for us
you turn the darkness of death
into the dawn of new life.
Show compassion to your people in their sorrow.

Be our refuge and our strength
to lift us from the darkness of this grief
to the peace and light of your presence.

Your son, our Lord Jesus Christ,
by dying for us, conquered death
and by rising again, restored life.

May we then go forward eagerly to meet him,
and after our life on earth
be reunited with our brothers and sisters
where every tear will be wiped away.

*Pastoral Care
of the Sick*

Y OU are the author and sustainer of our lives, O God,
you are our final home.
We commend to you N., our child.

Trusting in your mercy
and in your all-embracing love,
we pray that you give him/her happiness for ever.

Turn also to us who have suffered this loss.
Strengthen the bonds of this family and our community.
Confirm us in faith, in hope, and in love,
so that we may bear your peace to one another
and one day stand together with all the saints
who praise you for your saving help.

*Order of Christian
Funerals*

ONE may know perfectly well the statistical possibilities concerning natural disasters, freak accidents, and life-threatening diseases and regard these—theoretically, at least—as fully natural phenomena. But when such events suddenly threaten (or spare) one's own life, questions occur, so to speak, in the first person. One asks not what *caused* the earthquake, fire, or disease (for this may be obvious enough) but "Why did this happen now, in this way, to this person?"

Elaine Pagels

LORD,
N. is gone now from this earthly dwelling
and has left behind those who mourn his/her absence.
Grant that as we grieve for our brother/sister
we may hold his/her memory dear
and live in hope of the eternal kingdom
where you will bring us together again.

*Order of Christian
Funerals*

IF thou didst ever hold me in thy heart,
Absent thee from felicity awhile,
And in this harsh world draw thy breath in pain,
To tell my story.

*William Shakespeare
Sixteenth century*

MAY the love of God and the peace of the Lord Jesus Christ
bless and console us
and gently wipe every tear from our eyes:
in the name of the Father,
and of the Son, and of the Holy Spirit.

*Order of Christian
Funerals*

B EING a widow is like living in a country where nobody
speaks your language.

                                                                    Lynn Caine

O NCE in the time of the judges there was a famine in the
land; so a man from Bethlehem of Judah departed
with his wife and two sons to reside on the plateau of Moab.
The man was named Elimelech, his wife Naomi, and his
sons Mahlon and Chilion; they were Ephrathites from Bethlehem of Judah. Some time after their arrival on the Moabite
plateau, Elimelech, the husband of Naomi, died, and she
was left with her two sons, who married Moabite women,
one named Orpah, the other Ruth. When they had lived
there about ten years, both Mahlon and Chilion died also,
and the woman was left with neither her two sons nor her
husband. She then made ready to go back from the plateau
of Moab because word reached her there that the LORD had
visited his people and given them food.

She and her two daughters-in-law left the place where they
had been living. Then as they were on the road back to the
land of Judah, Naomi said to her two daughters-in-law, "Go
back, each of you, to your mother's house! May the LORD be
kind to you as you were to the departed and to me! May the
LORD grant each of you a husband and a home in which you
will find rest." She kissed them good-bye, but they wept with
loud sobs, and told her they would return with her to her
people. "Go back, my daughters!" said Naomi. "Why
should you come with me? Have I other sons in my womb
who may become your husbands? Go back, my daughters!
Go for I am too old to marry again. And even if I could offer
any hopes, or if tonight I had a husband or had borne sons,
would you then wait and deprive yourselves of husbands
until those sons grew up? No, my daughters! my lot is too
bitter for you, because the LORD has extended his hand
against me." Again they sobbed aloud and wept; and Orpah
kissed her mother-in-law good-bye, but Ruth stayed with
her.

"See now!" she said, "your sister-in-law has gone back to her people and her god. Go back after your sister-in-law!" But Ruth said, "Do not ask me to abandon or forsake you! for wherever you go I will go, wherever you lodge I will lodge, your people shall be my people, and your God my God. Wherever you die I will die, and there be buried. May the LORD do so and so to me, and more besides, if aught but death separates me from you!" Naomi then ceased to urge her, for she saw she was determined to go with her.

Ruth 1:1–8

I N the earliest attempts at the reform of our Catholic liturgy, as directed by Vatican II, the text of the Mass of Requiem, known from the first word of its entrance song, was replaced by a text called "the Mass of the Resurrection."

An important thing happened in the first blush of that liturgical change. People discovered that, with all the new emphasis on the hope for resurrection of the dead with Christ, mourners had no fitting ritual way to express their grief. The celebration of the joys of the last day, which no one but Jesus had experienced in their fullness, not even the blessed, was premature. The church's prayer was calling on people to rejoice and be glad, when at the moment their greatest need was to grieve.

And so, quietly, almost imperceptibly, after a year or two, the triumphant "Mass of the Resurrection" yielded to the more realistic "Mass of Christian Burial." Its prayers and readings are filled with faith, but they are less euphoric. The Lord will in the future wipe away the tears from every eye— but not now. The person who is dead has been totally freed from the power of sin—but we who live on have not! Jesus knew something of the glory he was called to—we simply do not. We do not know where our loved ones have been taken to and we want them back. The pain of separation is intense, as it was for Jesus' friends after they lost him. We may not forget that the eucharistic meal that we eat commemorates a departure: a wrenching, tearful separation.

Your grief is your own, all the days of your life. Let no one deprive you of it, not even out of love. Pain is inseparable from love; that is a truth we must live with. It is a proof of our true inner reality, a judgment of ourselves, as to how and with what courage we face and accept that truth.

Gerard S. Sloyan

THOUGH the mountains leave their place
and the hills be shaken,
My love shall never leave you
nor my covenant of peace be shaken,
says the LORD, who has mercy on you.

Isaiah 54:10

ROCK-A, my soul, in the bosom of Abraham,
Rock-a, my soul, in the bosom of Abraham,
Rock-a, my soul, in the bosom of Abraham,
Oh, rock-a, my soul.

American hymn

SUBVENITE, Sancti Dei,
occurite, Angeli Domini.
   Suscipientes animan ejus:
   Offerentes eam in conspectu Altissimi.
Suscipiat te Christus, qui vocat te:
et in sinum Abrahae Angeli deducant te.
   Suscipientes animam ejus:
   Offerentes eam in conspectu Altissimi.
Requiem aeternam dona ei, Domine:
et lux perpetua luceat ei.

Saints of God, come to their aid!
Hasten to meet them, angels of the Lord!
   Receive their souls and present them to God
      the Most High.
May Christ, who called you, take you to himself;
may angels lead you to the bosom of Abraham.
   Receive their souls and present them to God
      the Most High.
Eternal rest grant unto them, O Lord,
and let perpetual light shine upon them.

Catholic funeral rite

BUT your dead shall live, their corpses shall rise;
   awake and sing, you who lie in the dust.
For your dew is a dew of light,
   and the land of shades gives birth.

Isaiah 26:19

D EATH blessings vary in words but not in spirit. These death blessings are known by various names, as: Death Blessing, Soul Leading, Soul Peace, and other names familiar to the people.

The soul peace is intoned, not necessarily by a cleric, over the dying, and the man or the woman who says it is called soul-friend. He or she is held in special affection by the friends of the dying person ever after. The soul peace is slowly sung—all present earnestly joining the soul-friend in beseeching the three persons of the godhead and all the saints of heaven to receive the departing soul of earth. During the prayer the soul-friend makes the sign of the cross with the right thumb over the lips of the dying.

Be this soul on thine own arm, O Christ,
Thou King of the city of heaven,
And since thine it was, O Christ, to buy the soul,
At the time of the balancing of the beam,
At the time of the bringing in the judgment,
Be it now on thine own right hand,
    Oh! on thine own right hand.

And be the holy Michael, king of angels,
Coming to meet the soul,
And leading it home
To the heaven of the Son of God.
    The Holy Michael, high king of angels,
    Coming to meet the soul,
    And leading it home
    To the heaven of the Son of God.   Alexander Carmichael

O N the day of judgment when you will reward all according to their deeds, we beseech you, O Lord God, to make worthy the faithful departed who received you, the food of life, to meet you with joyful countenance.

May they rest in your heavenly mansions of light and joy, the heavenly Jerusalem, the city of the saints, with Abraham, Isaac and Jacob. Honor their memory on your altar; and when you gather us with them grant us the happiness that you have promised to the faithful; glory and honor are due to you now and forever.

Maronite liturgy

To you, O Lord,
   we humbly entrust this child,
so precious in your sight.
Take him/her into your arms
and welcome him/her into paradise,
where there will be no sorrow, no weeping nor pain,
but the fullness of peace and joy
with your Son and the Holy Spirit
for ever and ever.

*Order of Christian
Funerals*

INTO your hands, Father of mercies,
   we commend our brother/sister N.
in the sure and certain hope
that, together with all who have died in Christ,
he/she will rise with him on the last day.

Merciful Lord,
turn toward us and listen to our prayers:
open the gates of paradise to your servant
and help us who remain
to comfort one another with assurances of faith,
until we all meet in Christ
and are with you and with our brother/sister for ever.

*Order of Christian
Funerals*

I know that my Redeemer lives:
on the last day I shall rise again.
And in my flesh I shall see God.

I shall see him myself, face to face;
and my own eyes shall behold my Savior.

Within my heart this hope I cherish:
that in my flesh I shall see God.

*Order of Christian
Funerals*

OH, would that my words were
written down!
Would that they were inscribed in a record:
That with an iron chisel and with lead
    they were cut in the rock forever!
But as for me, I know that my Vindicator lives,
    and that he will at last stand forth upon the dust;
Whom I myself shall see:
    my own eyes, not another's shall behold him,
And from my flesh I shall see God;
    my inmost being is consumed with longing.

Job 19:23–26

GOD of loving kindness,
listen favorably to our prayers:
strengthen our belief that your Son has risen from the dead
and our hope that your servant N. will also rise again.

*Order of Christian
Funerals*

THIS world is not conclusion;
A sequel stands beyond,
Invisible, as music,
But positive, as sound.

Emily Dickinson
Nineteenth century

IN sickness, not only are we tormented by pain and by advancing deterioration of the body, but even more so by a dread of perpetual extinction. We rightly follow the intuition of our heart when we abhor and repudiate the absolute ruin and total disappearance of our own person.

The Church in the Modern World
Vatican II

DELIVER us from all evil, O God,
for we would not lose hope,
would not forget your love.
Love this child forever
as we have loved him/her.
Guide our steps now in ways of peace
till with our eyes we shall behold you
and shall praise you with all the saints
for ever and ever.

Gabe Huck

WE do not want you to be unaware about those who have fallen asleep, so that you may not grieve like the rest who have no hope. For if we believe that Jesus died and rose, so too will God, through Jesus, bring with him those who have fallen asleep.

1 Thessalonians
4:13–14

STANDING by the parking-ramp elevator
a week ago, sunk, stupid with sadness.
Black slush puddled on the cement floor,
the place painted a killer-pastel
as in an asylum.
A numeral 1, big as a person,
was stenciled on the cinder block:
Remember your level.
The toneless bell sounded.
Doors opened, nobody inside.
Then, who knows why, a rod of light
at the base of my skull flashed
to every outpost of my far-flung body—
I've got my life back.
It was nothing, just the present moment
occurring for the first time in months.
My head translated light,
my eyes spiked with tears.
The awful green walls, I could have stroked them.
The dirt, the moving cube I stepped into—
it was all beautiful,
everything that took me up.   Patricia Hampl

LET us observe, beloved, how the Ruler is continually
displaying the resurrection that will be, of which God
made the first fruits in raising the Lord Jesus Christ from the
dead. Let us look, beloved, at the resurrection which happens regularly. Day and night show us a resurrection; the
night goes to sleep, the day rises: the day departs, night
comes on. Let us take the crops. How does the sowing
happen, and in what way? "The sower went out" and cast
each of the seeds into the ground. These fall dry and bare on
the ground and decay. Then from the decay the mightiness of
the Ruler's providence raises them up, and many grow from   Clement of Rome
the one and bear fruit.   First century

A<small>T</small> daybreak on the first day of the week they took the spices they had prepared and went to the tomb. They found the stone rolled away from the tomb; but when they entered, they did not find the body of the Lord Jesus. While they were puzzling over this, behold, two men in dazzling garments appeared to them. They were terrified and bowed their faces to the ground. They said to them, "Why do you seek the living one among the dead? He is not here, but he has been raised. Remember what he said to you while he was still in Galilee, that the Son of Man must be handed over to the sinners and be crucified, and rise on the third day." And they remembered his words.

Luke 24:1–8

S URELY God knows how we were made,
And recalls that we are dust!
Our human life is a reed,
  A flower that blooms in the meadow.
It is gone when the wind blows over it;
  Its place recalls it no more.
But the grace of the Lord is eternal,
  Resting forever on those who fear God.
God's justice belongs to their offspring,
  To all who keep the covenant;
    Who remember to do what God commands.

Psalm 103:15–18

M R. Head stood very still and felt the action of mercy touch him again, but this time he knew that there were no words in the world that could name it. He understood that it grew out of agony, which is not denied to any man and which is given in strange ways to children. He understood it was all a man could carry into death to give his Maker, and he suddenly burned with shame that he had so little of it to take with him. He stood appalled, judging himself with the thoroughness of God, while the action of mercy covered his pride like a flame and consumed it. . . . He saw that no sin was too monstrous for him to claim as his own, and since God loved in proportion as He forgave, he felt ready at that instant to enter Paradise.

Flannery O'Connor

G OD, lover of souls,
you hold dear what you have made
and spare all things, for they are yours.
Look gently on your servant N.,
and by the blood of the cross
forgive his/her sins and failings.

Remember the faith of those who mourn
and satisfy their longing for that day
when all will be made new again
in Christ, our risen Lord,
who lives and reigns with you for ever and ever.

Order of Christian Funerals

O LORD Jesus Christ, King of glory, deliver the souls of all the faithful departed from the pains of hell and from the deep pit: deliver them from the lion's mouth, that hell may not swallow them up, and may they not fall into darkness; may your holy standard-bearer Michael lead them into the holy light; which you promised to Abraham and to his seed.

Offertory
Requiem Mass

S OON afterward Jesus journeyed to a city called Nain, and his disciples and a large crowd accompanied him. As he drew near to the gate of the city, a man who had died was being carried out, the only son of his mother, and she was a widow. A large crowd from the city was with her. When the Lord saw her, he was moved with pity for her and said to her, "Do not weep." He stepped forward and touched the coffin; at this the bearers halted, and he said, "Young man, I tell you, arise!" The dead man sat up and began to speak, and Jesus gave him to his mother. Fear seized them all, and they glorified God, exclaiming, "A great prophet has arisen in our midst," and "God has visited his people."

Luke 7:11–16

LORD Jesus, our Redeemer,
you willingly gave yourself up to death,
so that all might be saved and pass from death to life.
We humbly ask you to comfort your servants in their grief
and to receive N. into the arms of your mercy.
You alone are the Holy One,
you are mercy itself;
by dying you unlocked the gates of life
    for those who believe in you.
Forgive N. his/her sins,
and grant him/her a place of happiness, light, and peace
in the kingdom of your glory for ever and ever.

Order of Christian
Funerals

A PORTA inferi
erue, Domine, animam ejus.

From the gate of hell
deliver this soul, O Lord.

Catholic funeral rite

COME to me, all you who labor and are burdened, and I
will give you rest. Take my yoke upon you and learn
from me, for I am meek and humble of heart; and you will
find rest for yourselves. For my yoke is easy, and my burden
light.

Matthew 11:28–30

ARE you unaware that we who were baptized into Christ Jesus were baptized into his death? We were indeed buried with him through baptism into death, so that, just as Christ was raised from the dead by the glory of the Father, we too might live in newness of life.

For if we have grown into union with him through a death like his, we shall also be united with him in the resurrection. We know that our old self was crucified with him, so that our sinful body might be done away with, that we might no longer be in slavery to sin. For a dead person has been absolved from sin. If, then, we have died with Christ, we believe that we shall also live with him. We know that Christ, raised from the dead, dies no more; death no longer has power over him. As to his death, he died to sin once and for all; as to his life, he lives for God. Consequently, you too must think of yourself as being dead to sin and living for God in Christ Jesus.

Romans 6:3–11

YOU have become a new creation
and have clothed yourselves in Christ.
Receive this baptismal garment
and bring it unstained to the judgment seat
of our Lord Jesus Christ,
so that you may have everlasting life.

Catholic baptismal rite

YOU have been enlightened by Christ.
Walk always as children of the light
and keep the flame of faith alive in your hearts.
When the Lord comes, may you go out to meet him
with all the saints in the heavenly kingdom.

Catholic baptismal rite

GOD has made for us two kinds of eyes: those of flesh and those of faith. When you come to the sacred initiation, the eyes of the flesh see water; the eyes of faith behold the Spirit. Those eyes see the body being baptized; these eyes see the old existence being buried.

John Chrysostom
Fourth century

W E now find ourselves without a living tradition of rich baptismal art and discourse when it comes to understanding and implementing a far-reaching restoration of initiatory liturgy in our day. If you doubt this, look carefully at (or for) the fonts and baptistries in our churches. Note also the remarkable differences in the way we celebrate Christmas and Easter—Christmas with well-attended midnight Masses, Easter with poorly attended Vigils, which in most places must begin in the early evening, so that people, for some reason, will not have to be out late. This suggests that we have a vigorous, but largely sentimental and nostalgic, piety of Jesus the baby, but little piety of what this baby accomplished when he finally brought us home to his Father, trampling Death by his death. Lacking the latter, the former piety looks more like a function of civil religion than of the gospel.

. . . [We are] rendered deaf and blind to [our tradition's] baptismal images, such as standing in great peril (being swallowed whole by some horror from the deep, eaten by lions, betrayed by colleagues, reviled by the jeers of the unclean, and so on), and to great baptismal figures, such as Jonah, Esther, Moses, Israel escaping from Pharaoh through the Red Sea, Daniel, the three young men in the fiery furnace, John the Baptist, and finally Jesus the Christ, to name only a few. . . .

But *with* such images and figures we are forced to think much harder about the very heart of conversion and its costs, and we can see more clearly that the life that baptism throws open to us issues from the very core of reality itself— if we are first brave enough to die to that existential constriction and minimalism known as sin. Otherwise we are adolescents staring at the Sistine Chapel ceiling without knowing the God of Genesis, the patriarchs, Sybils and prophets. It's all just a video tape without the music.   Aidan Kavanagh

Spoken while the
pall is placed on
the coffin, 1969
Catholic funeral rite

O N the day of his/her baptism, N. put on Christ. In the day of Christ's coming, may he/she be clothed with glory.

F OR you have died, and your life is hidden with Christ in God. When Christ your life appears, then you too will appear with him in glory.

Colossians 3:3–4

T HE primary image for Christians, the image that colors all other reality, is the new exodus, the death and resurrection of Christ, which delivers them from the slavery of death and leads them to the promised land of God's kingdom. That event creates them as a people and gives them life.

Baptism is the people's entrance into that saving event, their passage through the waters of death into life. Paul says in the letter to the Romans, "Did you not know that all of us, when we were baptized into Christ Jesus, were baptized into his death? By our baptism into his death we were buried with him, so that as Christ was raised from the dead by the Father's glorious power, we too should begin living a new life" (Romans 6:3–4).

As Christians, we stand with death before us and behind us. We look back to the death of sin; we look ahead at the waters of baptism beyond which lies the promised land. Only through the waters of chaos, the waters of flood, the waters of the sea, can we come to life. Only through the waters of baptism can we become a new people. Only through baptism into Christ's death can we hope for a share in the resurrection. Water is a symbol of death; water is a symbol of life. Water has become our way through death to life.

Irene Nowell

G IVE rest, O Christ,
to your servant with your saints:
where sorrow and pain are no more;
neither sighing, but life everlasting.
You only are immortal,
the creator and maker of humankind:
and we are mortal, formed of the earth,
and unto earth shall we return:
for so you did ordain,
when thou created me, saying,
"Dust you are, and unto dust shall you return."
All we go down to the dust;
and weeping over the grave,
we make our song:
alleluia, alleluia, alleluia.

Orthodox liturgy
Thirteenth century

P ASCHAL mystery" and "everlasting life" are thus not
merely images that provide Christian content to the
coping rituals and grief therapy of people who happen to
call themselves Christians. These are images that proclaim
the very bedrock of Christian faith. The sooner Christians
recognize that the therapeutic value of their funeral rites
rests on this bedrock of faith in Jesus dead and risen, the
sooner will their funerals once again become both authen-
tically Christian and genuinely human ritual with an appro-
priate therapeutic value of their own.

Richard Rutherford

HOW often our own ministry of kingdom-building, of comparing the status quo with the possibilities the reign of God offers us, puts us somewhere between being run out of town and being led to the brow of the hill to be cast over the edge. The only hope in all of this, a hope most fully expressed and made present at liturgy, is the promise of Jesus that giving one's self fully for others means a passage from death to life—that death is indeed overcome, as well as anything that has to do with death: racism, sexism, militarism, the arms race, sickness, poverty, hatred, oppression of

Raymond Hunthausen   every sort.

AND thou, Jesus sweet Lord,
Art thou not also a mother?
Truly, thou art a mother,
The mother of all mothers,

Anselm   Who tasted death,
Eleventh century   In thy desire to give life to thy children.

WHAT Thérèse experienced at the moment of her death cannot be known. But by the time of her death she attached no importance to either ecstasy or any other experience described by a saint or connected with the death of a saint. She didn't expect it, she didn't anticipate it, and she warned her sisters explicitly against looking for "anything extraordinary" at her death. By the end of her life Thérèse had no need to look to saints or to any imagined idea for guidelines. She identified completely with one person, Jesus—the spotless victim who redeemed others by his act

Patricia O'Connor   of love and who died in agony.

I T would be a great mistake to think of secularism as simply an "absence of religion." It is, in fact, itself a religion, and as such, an explanation of death and a reconciliation with it. It is the religion of those who are tired of having the world explained in terms of "other world" of which no one knows anything, and life explained in terms of a "survival" about which no one has the slightest idea; tired of having, in other words, life given "value" in terms of death. Secularism is an "explanation" of death in terms of life. The only world we know is this world, the only life given to us is this life—and it is up to us to make it as meaningful, as rich, as happy as possible. Life ends with death. This is unpleasant, but since it is natural, since death is a universal phenomenon, the best thing we can do about it, is simply to accept it as something natural. . . .

The purpose of Christianity is not to help people by reconciling them to death, but to reveal the Truth about life and death in order that people may be saved by this Truth. Salvation, however, is not only not identical with help, but is, in fact, opposed to it. Christianity quarrels with religion and secularism not because they offer "insufficient help," but precisely because they "suffice," because they "satisfy" our needs. If the purpose of Christianity were to take away from us the fear of death, to reconcile us with death, there would be no need for Christianity, for each religion has done this, indeed, better than Christianity. . . .

Christianity is not reconciliation with death. It is the revelation of death, and it reveals death because it is the revelation of Life. Christ is this Life. And only if Christ is Life is death what Christianity proclaims it to be, namely the enemy to be destroyed, and not a "mystery" to be explained. Religion and secularism by explaining death give it a "status," a rationale, make it "normal." Only Christianity proclaims it to be *abnormal* and, therefore, truly horrible. At the grave of Lazarus Christ wept. . . .

The liturgy of Christian death does not begin when a person has come to the inescapable end and the corpse lies in church for the last rites while we stand around, the sad yet resigned witnesses of the dignified removal of a person from the world of the living. It begins every Sunday as the church ascending into heaven, "puts aside all earthly care"; it begins every feast day; it begins especially in the joy of Easter. . . .

The preaching of the resurrection remains foolishness to this world and no wonder even Christians themselves somehow "explain it away" by virtually reducing it to the old pre-Christian doctrines of immortality and survival. And indeed, if the doctrine of resurrection is just a "doctrine," if it is to be believed in as an event of the "future," as a mystery of the "other world," it is not substantially different from the other doctrines concerning the "other world" and can be easily confused with them. Whether it is the immortality of the soul or the resurrection of the body—I know nothing of them and all discussion here is mere "speculation." Death remains the same mysterious passage into a mysterious future. The *great joy* that the disciples felt when they saw the risen Lord, this "burning of heart" that they experienced on the way to Emmaus was not because the mysteries of an "other world" were revealed to them. It was *because* they saw the Lord. And he sent them to preach and to proclaim not the resurrection of the dead—not a doctrine of death—but repentance and remission of sins, the new life, the kingdom. They announced what they knew, that in Christ the *new life* has already begun, that he is Life Eternal, the Fulfillment, the Resurrection and the Joy of the world.

The church is the entrance into the risen life of Christ, communion in life eternal, "joy and peace in the Holy Spirit." And it is the expectation of the "day without evening" of the kingdom; not of any "other world," but of the fulfillment of all things and all life in Christ. In him death itself has become an act of life, for he has filled it with himself, with his love and light. In him "all things are yours; whether . . . the world, or life, or death, or things present, or things to come; all are yours; and you are Christ's; and Christ is God's" (1 Corinthians 3:21–23). And if I make this *new life* mine, mine this hunger and thirst of the kingdom, mine this expectation of Christ, mine the certitude that Christ is Life, my very death will be an act of communion with Life.

For neither life nor death can separate us from the love of Christ. I do not know when and how the fulfillment will come. I do not know when all things will be consummated in Christ. I know nothing about the "whens" and "hows." But I know that in Christ this great Passage, the *Pascha* of the world has begun, that the light of the "world to come" comes to us in the joy and peace of the Holy Spirit, for *Christ is risen and Life reigneth.*

Alexander Schmemann

B LESSED be the God and Father of our Lord Jesus Christ, who in his great mercy gave us a new birth to a living hope through the resurrection of Jesus Christ from the dead, to an inheritance that is imperishable, undefiled, and unfading, kept in heaven for you who by the power of God are safeguarded through faith, to a salvation that is ready to be revealed in the final time.

1 Peter 1:3–5

G OD did not destine us for wrath, but to gain salvation through our Lord Jesus Christ, who died for us, so that whether we are awake or asleep, we may live together with him. Therefore, encourage one another and build one another up, as indeed you do.

1 Thessalonians
5:9–11

N EARER, my God, to thee,
Nearer to thee!
E'en tho' it be a cross
That raiseth me;
Still all my song shall be,

Nearer, my God, to thee,
Nearer, my God, to thee,
Nearer to thee!

Sarah Adams
Nineteenth century

Apostles' Creed

H E descended to the dead.

CHRIST has gone to search for our first parent, as for a lost sheep. Greatly desiring to visit those who live in darkness and in the shadow of death, he has gone to free from sorrow the captives Adam and Eve, he who is both God and the son of Eve. The Lord approached them bearing the cross, the weapon that had won him the victory. At the sight of him Adam, the first man he had created, struck his breast in terror and cried out to everyone: "My Lord be with you all." Christ answered him: "And with your spirit." He took him by the hand and raised him up, saying, "Awake, O sleeper, and rise from the dead, and Christ will give you light."

Rise, let us leave this place. The enemy led you out of the earthly paradise. I will not restore you to that paradise, but I will enthrone you in heaven. I forbade you the tree that was only a symbol of life, but see, I who am life itself am now one with you. I appointed cherubim to guard you as slaves are guarded, but now I make them worship you as God. The throne formed by cherubim awaits you, its bearer swift and eager. The bridal chamber is adorned, the banquet is ready, the eternal dwelling places are prepared, the treasure houses of all good things lie open. The kingdom of heaven has been prepared for you from all eternity.

From an ancient homily, Office of Readings, Holy Saturday Roman rite

O deathless One! To those in darkness you appeared, raising fallen people. O you, our redeemer and our light! All glory be yours forever.

Orthodox liturgy

A LMIGHTY God,
through the death of your Son on the cross
you destroyed our death;
through his rest in the tomb
you hallowed the graves of all who believe in you;
and through his rising again
you restored us to eternal life.

God of the living and the dead,
accept our prayers
for those who have died in Christ
and are buried with him in the hope of rising again.
Since they were true to your name on earth,   *Order of Christian*
let them praise you for ever in the joy of heaven.   *Funerals*

L ORD, lead me out of the ways of darkness; you broke
down the gates of death, and visited the prisoners of
darkness; you brought them light to let them see your face.
They cried out in welcome: "Redeemer, you have come at   Catholic funeral
last!"   liturgy, 1969 rite

I N speaking of the death of Christ on the cross, Ephrem and
the Syriac writers are aware continually of his abiding
divinity. Ephrem in his *Hymn on the Unleavened Bread*
expresses the paradox:
   It is by the power which comes from him
   that the wood bore him;
   and the wood was not burnt
   even though it carried fire!
[Elsewhere Ephrem writes:]
   The Merciful one has looked down
      and has seen the soul in the abyss
   and has opened a way for it to extricate itself

Even if a simple sign on his part would suffice.
He has imprinted his love on his work,
    in putting on humanity;
Then he appropriated human ignorance to lead humans
    to his knowledge.
He has chanted to humans on his harp his humble chants
so that humans be raised to the heights;
He has raised his cross toward the heights
so that the children of Eve climb
    toward the heavenly beings.

It is the descent into sheol that completes the work of redemption. The kingdom of death must be defeated and deceased humans, especially Adam, must be liberated and recovered. James of Serug influenced by Philippians 2:16 usually speaks of the Son of God who has the appearance of a servant and is not recognized by the demons because of his humility and suffering. Christ's true identity is revealed in the crucifixion. By his descent into sheol, he triumphs over the empire of death and gloriously returns to the Father in the company of liberated prisoners.

James of Serug has Christ seeking the lost Adam even on the occasion of his baptism. He presents Christ as saying to John the Baptizer: "I am trying to find the lost Adam; let me go down and look for Adam." In fact, Christ's baptism and the descent into sheol are often considered together.

The descent into sheol is the principal image used by the Syriac Fathers to describe the cosmic struggle between Christ, who ultimately is the creator of life, and the power of death and sin. Jesus by the instrumentality of the cross had to overcome the "dragon-serpent." Humanity left to itself, in which sin reigned, was incapable of overcoming the dragon. It is Christ, the victorious king and son of David, who by his glorious cross has reduced the powerful evil one to silence.

For the Syriac Fathers, the action of Christ's descent into sheol becomes a guarantee of life and resurrection for all humans. Ephrem observes that only Christ could go to a place from where no one could come out, and then come forth without any power being able to hinder him.

Seely Beggiani

I N sure and certain hope of the resurrection
to eternal life
through our Lord Jesus Christ,
we commend to Almighty God our brother/sister N.,
and we commit his/her body to the ground
   [*or* the deep *or* the elements *or* its resting place]:
earth to earth, ashes to ashes, dust to dust.

The Lord bless him/her and keep him/her,
the Lord make his face to shine upon him/her
   and be gracious to him/her,
the Lord lift up his countenance upon him/her
   and give him/her peace. ·

*Book of Common
Prayer*

T HE old men used to sing
And lifted a brother
Carefully
Out the door
I used to think they
Were born
Knowing how to
Gently swing
A casket
They shuffled softly
Eyes dry
   More awkward
With the flowers
Than with the widow
After they'd put the
Body in
And stood around waiting
In their
Brown suits.

Alice Walker

ALL praise to you, Lord of all creation.
Praise to you, holy and living God.
We praise and bless you for your mercy,
we praise and bless you for your kindness.
Blessed is the Lord, our God.

Blessed is the Lord, our God.

You sanctify the homes of the living
and make holy the places of the dead.
You alone open the gates of righteousness
and lead us to the dwellings of the saints.
Blessed is the Lord, our God.

Blessed is the Lord, our God.

We praise you, our refuge and strength.
We bless you, our God and Redeemer.
Your praise is always in our hearts and on our lips.
We remember the mighty deeds of the covenant.
Blessed is the Lord, our God.

Blessed is the Lord, our God.

Almighty and ever-living God,
remember the mercy with which you graced your
        servant N. in life.
Receive him/her, we pray, into the mansions of the saints.
As we make ready our brother's/sister's resting place,
Order of Christian look also with favor on those who mourn
Funerals and comfort them in their loss.

JOSEPH took Jesus down, wrapped him in the linen cloth,
and laid him in a tomb that had been hewn out of the
Mark 15:46 rock.

P EACE be with those who have left us and have gone
to God. May they be at peace. May they be with God.

May they be with the living God.
May they be with the immortal God.
May they be in God's hands.

May they sleep in peace.
May they live in peace.
May they be where the name of God is great.

May they be with the living God now and on the day
    of judgment.
May they live with God.
May they live in eternal light.

May they live in the peace of the Lord.
May they live forever in peace.
With God in peace.

Catholic funeral liturgy,
1969 rite

O gaping earth!
Receive the body formed of you by the hand of God
    and again returning to you as its mother;
for what has been to his image, the Creator has already
    reclaimed,
Receive then this as your own.

Orthodox liturgy

NOW I lay me down to sleep,
I pray the Lord my soul to keep.
Four corners to my bed,
Four angels there aspread:
Two to foot and two to head,
And four to carry me when I'm dead.
If any danger come to me,
Sweet Jesus Christ, deliver me.
And if I die before I wake,
Old English prayer   I pray the Lord my soul to take.

MAY God open to me every pass,
Christ open to me every narrow way,
each soul of holy man and woman in heaven,
be preparing for me
Celtic prayer   my pathway.

IN thy name, O Jesu
Who wast crucified,
I lie down to rest.

Watch thou me
in sleep remote,
hold thou me
in thy one hand;
Watch thou me
in sleep remote,
hold thou me
Celtic prayer   in thy one hand.

THE eighteenth-century Hasidic Jews had more sense, and more belief. One Hasidic slaughterer, whose work required invoking the Lord, bade a tearful farewell to his wife and children every morning before he set out for the slaughterhouse. He felt, every morning, that he would never see any of them again. For every day, as he himself stood with his knife in his hands, the words of his prayer carried him into danger. After he called on God, God might notice and destroy him before he had time to utter the rest, "Have mercy."

Another Hasid, a rabbi, refused to promise a friend to visit him the next day: "How can you ask me to make such a promise? This evening I must pray and recite 'Hear, O Israel.' When I say these words, my soul goes out to the utmost rim of life. . . . Perhaps I shall not die this time either, but how can I now promise to do something at a time after the prayer?"

Annie Dillard

ALL praise to thee, my God, this night,
For all the blessings of the light;
Keep me, O keep me, King of kings,
Beneath thine own almighty wings.

Forgive me, Lord, for thy dear Son,
The sin that I this day have done,
That with the world, myself and thee,
I, before sleep, at peace may be.

Teach me to live that I may dread
The grave as little as my bed;
Teach me to die that so I may
Rise glorious on that final day.

Thomas Ken
Nineteenth century

HOWEVER blind life or the spiral may be, there is an hour when it all stops. . . . What then will we need? We no longer share a vision of the good death. Most other cultures, including many primitive ones whom we have subjugated to our reason and our technology, enfold their members in an art of dying as in an art of living. But we have left these awesome tasks of culture to private choice. . . . We have created a new need, the need to live an examined life; we pursue its satisfaction in the full babble of conflicting opinions about what life is for, and we pursue it in a collectively held silence about the meaning of death.

Michael Isnatieff

GOD be in my hede
    And in my understandyng,
God be in myne eyes
    And in my loking,
God be in my mouth
    And in my speaking.
God be in my harte
    And in my thynkyng,
God be at mine ende
    And at my departyng.

Old English prayer

O God, whose days are without end, and whose mercies cannot be numbered: Make us, we pray, deeply aware of the shortness and uncertainty of human life; and let your Holy Spirit lead us in holiness and righteousness all our days; that, when we shall have served you in our generation, we may be gathered to our ancestors, having the testimony of a good conscience, in the communion of the Catholic Church, in the confidence of a certain faith, in the comfort of a religious and holy hope, in favor with you, our God, and in perfect charity with the world.

Book of Common
Prayer

THE day is past and gone,
The evening shades appear;
O may we all remember well,
The night of death is near.

We lay our garments by,
Upon our beds to rest:
So death will soon disrobe us all
Of what we here possess.

Lord, keep us safe this night,
Secure from all our fears:
May angels guard us while we sleep,
Till morning light appears.

And when we early rise,
And view th' unwearied sun,
May we set out to win the prize,
And after glory run.

And when our days are past,
And we from time remove,
O may we in thy bosom rest,
The bosom of thy love.

Baptist Harmony

MAY the all-powerful Lord grant us
a restful night
and a peaceful death.

Night prayer

Dies irae, dies illa,
Solvet saeclum in favilla:
Teste David cum Sibylla.

Quantus tremor est futurus,
Quando judex est venturus
Cuncta stricte discussurus!

Tuba mirum spargens sonum
Per sepulcra regionum,
Coget omnes ante thronum.

Mors stupebit, et natura,
Cum resurget creatura,
Judicanti responsura. . . .

Rex tremendae majestatis,
Qui salvandos salvas gratis,
Salva me, fons pietatis.

Recordare, Jesu pie,
Quod sum causa tuae viae:
Ne me perdas illa die. . . .

Qui Mariam absolvisti,
Et latronem exaudisti,
Mihi quoque spem dedisti. . . .

Inter oves locum praesta,
Et ab haedis me sequestra,
Statuens in parte dextra.

Confutatis maledictis,
Flammis acribus addictis:
Voca me cum benedictis.

Oro supplex et acclinis,
Cor contritum quasi cinis:
Gere curam mei finis.

Lacrimosa dies illa,
Qua resurget ex favilla
Judicandus homo reus
Huic ergo parce Deus.

Pie Jesu Domine, dona eis requiem.
Amen.

Sequence, First
Sunday of Advent
Twelfth century

HEAR'ST thou, my soul, what serious things
Both the Psalm and Sibyl sings
Of a sure Judge, from whose sharp ray
The world in flames shall fly away!

O that Fire! before whose face
Heaven and earth shall find no place:
O those Eyes! whose angry light
Must be the day of that dread night.

O that Trump! whose blast shall run
An even round with th' circling Sun,
And urge the murmuring graves to bring
Pale humans forth to meet their King.

Horror of Nature, Hell, and Death!
When a deep groan from beneath
Shall cry, "We come, we come!" and all
The caves of night answer one call.

O that book! whose leaves so bright
Will set the world in severe light.
O that Judge! whose hand, whose eye
None can endure, yet none can fly.

Ah then, poor soul! what wilt thou say?
And to what patron choose to pray,
When the stars themselves shall stagger, and
The most firm foot no more then stand?

But thou giv'st leave, dread Lord, that we
Take shelter from thyself in thee;
And with the wings of thine own dove
Fly to thy scepter of soft love!

Dear Lord, remember in that day
Who was the cause thou cam'st this way;
Thy sheep was strayed, and thou would'st be
Even lost thyself in seeking me! . . .

Just mercy, then, thy reck'ning be
With my price, and not with me;
'Twas paid at first with too much pain
To be paid twice, or once in vain.

Mercy, my Judge, mercy I cry,
With blushing cheek and bleeding eye;
The conscious colors of my sin
Are red without, and pale within.

O let thine own soft bowels pay
Thyself, and so discharge that day!
If Sin can sigh, Love can forgive,
O, say the word, my soul shall live!

Those mercies which thy Mary found,
Or who thy cross confess'd and crowned,
Hope tells my heart the same loves be
Still alive, and still for me.

Though both my prayers and tears combine,
Both worthless are, for they are mine;
But thou thy bounteous self still be,
And show thou art by saving me.

O when thy last frown shall proclaim
The flocks of goats to folds of flame,
And all thy lost sheep found shall be,
Let "Come ye blessed" then call me!

When the dread "Ite" shall divide
Those limbs of death from thy left side,
Let those life-speaking lips command
That I inherit thy right hand!

O, hear a suppliant heart all crush'd
And crumbled into contrite dust!
My hope, my fear—my Judge, my Friend!   Seventeenth century
Take charge of me, and of my end!   translation of "Dies Irae"
                                                           by Richard Crashaw

T HE Lord answered me and said:
        Write down the vision
Clearly upon the tablets,
    so that one can read it readily.
For the vision still has its time,
    presses on to fulfillment, and will not disappoint;
If it delays, wait for it,
    it will surely come, it will not be late.   Habakkuk 2:2–3

B EFORE his death, Rabbi Zusya said, "In the coming
     world, they will not ask me: 'Why were you not Moses?'
They will ask me: 'Why were you not Zusya?'"   Martin Buber

A<small>T</small> that time there shall arise
Michael, the great prince,
guardian of your people;
It shall be a time unsurpassed in distress
since nations began until that time.
At that time your people shall escape,
everyone who is found written in the book.
Many of those who sleep
in the dust of the earth shall awake;
Some shall live forever,
others shall be an everlasting horror and disgrace.
But the wise shall shine brightly
like the splendor of the firmament,
And those who lead the many to justice
Daniel 12:1–3   shall be like the stars forever.

I<small>F</small> ever my grief were measured
or my sorrow put on a scale,
it would outweigh the sands of the ocean.
For God has hidden my way
and put hedges across my path.

I sit and gnaw on my grief;
my groans pour out like water.
My worst fears have happened;
my nightmares have come to life.
Silence and peace have abandoned me,
Jewish prayer   and anguish camps in my heart.

T<small>HIS</small> ae night, this ae night,
Every night and alle,
Fire, and sleet, and candle light,
And Christ receive thy saule.

When thou from hence away are passed,
  Every night and alle,
To Whinny-muir thou comest at last,
  And Christ receive thy saule.

If ever thou gavest hosen and shoon,
  Every night and alle,
Sit thee down and put them on,
  And Christ receive thy saule.

If hosen and shoon thou ne'er gavest nane,
  Every night and alle,
The whinnies hall prick thee to the bare bane,
  And Christ receive thy saule.

From Whinny-muir when thou mayst pass,
  Every night and alle,
To Brigg o'Dread thou comest at last,
  And Christ receive thy saule.

From Brigg o'Dread when thou mayst pass,
  Every night and alle,
To purgatory fire thou comest at last,
  And Christ receive thy saule.

If ever thou gavest meat or drink,
  Every night and alle,
The fire shall never make thee shrink,
  And Christ receive thy saule.

If meat or drink thou never gavest nane,
  Every night and alle,
The fire will burn thee to the bare bane,
  And Christ receive thy saule.

This ae night, this ae night,
  Every night and alle,
Fire, and sleet, and candle light,
  And Christ receive thy saule.   Old English dirge

R EMEMBER, Lord, your church,
to deliver it from every evil,
and to make it perfect in your love.
  Praise to you now and evermore!

Gather together from the four winds
this sanctified church
into the kingdom that you have prepared.
  Praise to you now and evermore!

Come, Lord, and let this world pass!
  Amen.
Hosanna to the house of David!
  Amen.
Let those who are holy, come!
  Amen.
Let those who are not, repent!
  Amen.
Marana tha (Come, Lord)!
  Amen.

Didache
Second century

W E are much more concerned with the act of dying
than with being victorious over death. Socrates mas-
tered the art of dying: Christ overcame death as the last
enemy. . . . The one is within human capacity, the other
implies resurrection. We need not the art of dying but the
resurrection of Christ to invigorate and cleanse the world
today. . . . To live in the light of the resurrection—that is the
meaning of Easter. Do you not also find that few people seem
to know what light it is they live by? . . . It is an unconscious
waiting for the word of deliverance, though the time is
hardly ripe yet for it to be heard.

Dietrich Bonhoeffer

C OME, my Lord! Our darkness end!
 Break the bonds of time and space.
All the power of evil rend
By the radiance of your face.
The laughing stars with joy attend:
Come, Lord Jesus! Be my end!   Madeleine L'Engle

A MEN, I say to you, this generation will not pass away
 until all these things have taken place.   Matthew 24:34

I heard Death and Satan loudly disputing
 which was the strongest of the two.

DEATH

Only those who want to, O Evil One, listen to you,
but to me they come, whether they will or not.

SATAN

You just employ brute force, O Death,
whereas I use traps and cunning snares.

DEATH

Listen, Evil One, a cunning man can break your yoke,
but there is none who can escape from mine.

SATAN

You, Death, exercise your strength on the sick,
but I am the stronger with those who are well.

DEATH

You Evil One, go around like a hooligan,
whereas I am like a lion, fearlessly crushing my prey.

SATAN

You have no one who serves or worships you, O Death,
but me kings honor with sacrifices, like a god.

DEATH

But many address Death as a benefactor,
whereas no one ever has or shall call on you as such,
O Evil One.

SATAN

Do you not realize, Death, how many
call on me in one way or another, and offer me libations?

DEATH

Everyone fears me as a master,
but you they hate as the Evil One.

SATAN

People hate your name and your deeds, O Death:
my name may be hated, but my pleasures are loved.

CHORUS

Blessed is the one who set the accursed slaves against
     each other
so that we can laugh at them just as they laughed at us.
Our laughing at them now, my friends, is a pledge
that we shall again be enabled to laugh, at the
     resurrection.

REFRAIN

Praise to you, Son of the Shepherd of all, who has saved
     his flock
from the hidden wolves, the Evil One and Death.

Saint Ephrem,
Nisibeme Hymns
Fourth century

OH, when I come to die,
Oh, when I come to die,
Oh, when I come to die,
Give me Jesus.

In that mornin' when I rise,
That mornin' when I rise,
In that mornin' when I rise,
Give me Jesus.

Give me Jesus, give me Jesus,
You may have all this world, give me Jesus.
Oh, give me Jesus, give me Jesus,
You may have all this world, give me Jesus.

Dark midnight was my cry,
Dark midnight was my cry,
Dark midnight was my cry,
Give me Jesus.

I heard a mourner say,
I heard a mourner say,
I heard a mourner say,
Give me Jesus.

African-American
spiritual

MY purity intact for you, my lamp alight in my hand,
Bridegroom, I come out to meet you.
Not for me the pale joys,
the pleasures, loves, of an existence
fed with mortal pleasure.
I long for you to take me in your arms
and give me life;
I want to look at you forever,
my Blessed One, my Beauty.
    My purity intact for you, my lamp alight in my hand,
    Bridegroom, I come out to meet you.

Joy to you, Christ, Master of life's ballet,
Light of our days, undimmed at evening.
The virgins acclaim you; take what they bring you:
Flower of all flowers, our Love, our Joy,
Understanding, Wisdom, Word.
        My purity intact for you, my lamp alight in my hand,
        Bridegroom, I come out to meet you.
Stand by the open doors,
queen in the glittering gown;
bid us too welcome to the marriage room.
Virgin your body, bride,
splendid your victory,
sweet the scent of your breath.
See us now beside Christ,
dressed like you, ready to celebrate
your marriage, blest branch of God's olive.
        My purity intact for you, my lamp alight in my hand,
        Bridegroom, I come out to meet you.
Clear the colors Abel used
to paint your death before you died,
my Blessed.
Down streamed his blood,
his eyes sought heaven, as he said:
"My brother's hand has made this cruel wound.
Take me, Word, I beseech you."
        My purity intact for you, my lamp alight in my hand,
        Bridegroom, I come out to meet you.
John washed the crowds in the cleansing waters:
you were to wash them too.
A bad man sent him undeserved to death,
for purity.
Blood drenched the dust, but still he cried to you:
        My purity intact for you, my lamp alight in my hand,
        Bridegroom, I come out to meet you.

The mother, my Life that bore you
stood firm and fast in your grace.
The womb that held you, spotless Germ,
no man had sown with his seed.
Virgin she was, though seeming to betray
the marriage bed. Big with her blissful fruit she said:
>My purity intact for you, my lamp alight in my hand,
>Bridegroom, I come out to meet you.

We the bridesmaids
sing your praises,
happy woman, bride of God,
virgin still, Ecclesia.
Snow your body is, dark the waves of your hair,
sound, unblemished, lovely creature.
>My purity intact for you, my lamp alight in my hand,
>Bridegroom, I come out to meet you.

Decay is destroyed; disease,
with its pain and its tears, has gone.
Death is no more, folly has fled
and grief, that gnaws the mind,
is dead. A sudden shaft of joy
from Christ our God,
and now this mortal world is shining.
>My purity intact for you, my lamp alight in my hand,
>Bridegroom, I come out to meet you.

Blest Father, beginning never,
holding all things ever
in strength together,
taking the spotless heavens for your home:
may we too pass beyond the gates of life,
welcomed by you, O Father, and your Son.
>My purity intact for you, my lamp alight in my hand,
>Bridegroom, I come out to meet you.

Methodius of Olympus
Fourth century

Revelation 22:1–2

T HEN the angel showed me the river of life-giving water, sparkling like crystal, flowing from the throne of God and of the Lamb down the middle of its street. On either side of the river grew the tree of life that produces fruit twelve times a year, once each month; the leaves of the trees serve as medicine for the nations.

T HE body's participation in praise transfigures sensible beauty. No wonder that John of Patmos has inspired the orations and songs of so many musicians. John's images are filled with sensible content—with colors, sounds, smells (the prayers of the saints were in the seven bowls of incense), and things we can touch and taste (smooth white stones and seas like shining glass, fire that burns, the bitter taste of wormwood and the scroll that was sweet to eat, but bitter to digest). And John's vision is a cosmic one: before the throne of God all people and nations, tongues and kings are gathered to learn the measure of the two cities—the joy of abundant life, the terror and destruction of death, and the patience that endures. Here in this life and in our song is the open door, the opportunity, that John saw in the paradise of God: the body is our entry into God's sight, who alone is worthy of "power and wealth and might and wisdom and honor and glory and blessing" forever.

Rachel Reeder

O H! what a beautiful city,
Oh! what a beautiful city,
Oh! what a beautiful city,
Twelve gates to the city, Hallelu!

Three gates in the east,
Three gates in the west,
Three gates in the north,
And three gates in the south,
Making it twelve gates to the city, Hallelu!

African-American spiritual

I rejoiced because they said to me,
   "We will go up to the house of the LORD."
And now we have set foot
   within your gates, O Jerusalem—
Jerusalem, built as a city
   with compact unity.

To it the tribes go up
   the tribes of the LORD,
According to the decree for Israel,
   to give thanks to the name of the LORD.
In it are set up judgment seats,
   seats for the house of David.

Pray for the peace of Jerusalem!
   May those who love you prosper!
May peace be within your walls,
   prosperity in your buildings.
Because of my relatives and friends
   I will say, "Peace be within you!"
Because of the house of the LORD, our God,
   I will pray for your good.   Psalm 122

WE must stop this conspiracy of silence about death, and talk openly about it. One can go to church a whole lifetime and never hear a sermon on death.

If I were a young preacher again, I would preach the Christian gospel of eternal life in God, but I would preach it sooner in my ministry, preach it throughout, and I would preach it more realistically. The Bible really has nothing to say about eternal life. That sounds like a shocking statement, but it's literally true: There is not a single clear and concrete word in the Bible about life after death. It affirms that life with God is life with that which does not die. But any specification about life after death is steadily avoided by the biblical writers.

Paul made an effort to address the question, but its a bum effort: "What you sow does not come to life unless it dies. And what you sow is not the body which is to be, but a bare kernel, perhaps of wheat or of some other grain. But God gives it a body as he has chosen, and to each kind of seed its own body. For not all flesh is alike, but there is one kind for men, another for animals, another for birds, and another for fish" (1 Corinthians 15:36−39). He tries by natural analogy to say something. Interestingly, he never tried it again.

In Romans, the most mature of Paul's epistles, he says, "If we live, we live to the Lord, and if we die, we die to the Lord; so then, whether we live or whether we die, we are the Lord's" (Romans 14:8). Period! That is the fundamental and absolute word of scripture. But that word is immensely satisfying to old people. I never try to give any blueprints of eternity or heaven or eternal life, since by definition it is utterly impossible.

I think instead of trying to answer all the questions about death, we ought to follow the example of Paul and the New Testament and say, "Eye has not seen nor ear heard"; "By faith we are saved."

Josepth Sittler   By faith we are saved.

D EEP river,
   My home is over Jordan.
Deep river, Lord,
I want to cross over into campground.

Oh, don't you want to go
      to that gospel feast,
To that promised land
      where all is peace?

Oh, walk into heaven
   and claim your seat
And toss your crown
   at Jesus' feet.

African-American
spiritual

F IX me for my long white robe.
   Fix me, Jesus, fix me.
Fix me for my starry crown.
Fix me, Jesus, fix me.

   Oh, fix me;
   Oh, fix me;
   Oh, fix me;
   Fix me, Jesus, fix me.

Fix me for my journey home.
Fix me, Jesus, fix me.
Fix me for my dying bed.
Fix me, Jesus, fix me.

African-American
spiritual

LIGHT'S abode, celestial Salem,
vision whence true peace doth spring,
brighter than the heart can fancy,
mansion of the highest King;
O how glorious are the praises
which of thee the prophets sing!

There for ever and for ever
alleluia is outpoured;
for unending, for unbroken
is the feast day of the Lord;
all is pure and all is holy
that within thy walls is stored.

There no cloud nor passing vapor
dims the brightness of the air;
endless noonday, glorious noonday,
from the Sun of suns is there;
there no night brings rest from labor,
for unknown are toil and care.

O how glorious and resplendent,
fragile body, shalt thou be,
when endued with heavenly beauty,
full of health, and strong, and free,
full of vigor, full of pleasure
that shall last eternally!

Now with gladness, now with courage,
bear the burden on thee laid,
that hereafter these thy labors
may with endless gifts be paid,
and in everlasting glory
thou with brightness be arrayed.

Latin hymn
Fifteenth century

I looked over Jordan, and what did I see,
Coming for to carry me home?
A band of angels coming after me,
Coming for to carry me home.

  Swing low, sweet chariot,
  Coming for to carry me home,
  Swing low, sweet chariot,
  Coming for to carry me home.

If you get there before I do,
Coming for to carry me home,
Tell all my friends I'm coming too,
Coming for to carry me home.

I'm sometimes up, I'm sometimes down,
Coming for to carry me home,
But still my soul feels heavenly bound,
Coming for to carry me home.

African-American spiritual

INTO your hands, O Lord,
we humbly entrust our brother/sister N.
In this life you embraced him/her with your tender love;
deliver him/her now from every evil
and bid him/her to enter eternal rest.

The old order has passed away:
welcome him/her then into paradise,
where there will be no sorrow, no weeping nor pain,
but the fullness of peace and joy
with your Son and the Holy Spirit
for ever and ever.

Order of Christian Funerals

IN paradisum deducant te Angeli:
in tuo adventu suscipiant te Martyres,
et perducant te in civitatem sanctam Jerusalem.
Chorus Angelorum suscipiat,
et cum Lazaro quondam paupere aeternam habeas
    requiem.

May the angels lead you into paradise;
may the martyrs come to welcome you
and take you to the holy city,
the new and eternal Jerusalem.
May the choir of angels welcome you,
and where Lazarus is poor no longer
Catholic funeral rite   may you find eternal rest.

WE do not live to ourselves, and we do not die to
ourselves. If we live, we live to the Lord, and if we die,
we die to the Lord; so then, whether we live or whether we
die, we are the Lord's. For to this end Christ died and lived
Romans 14:7–9   again, so that he might be Lord of both the dead and the living.

CHRIST has risen from the dead,
Orthodox liturgy   trampling down death by death.

PER omnia saecula saeculorum.
Amen.

Endnotes

ALL SAINTS

Sing with: Music can be found in *Worship,* #467.

So we look: Adapted from "In the Company of the Faithful," Vincent Harding. Reprinted by permission of *Sojourners,* Washington, D.C.

Jerusalem: Music can be found in *Worship,* #690.

One of the tasks: From *Ritual and Pastoral Care,* Elaine Ramshaw. Copyright © 1987, Fortress Press. Reprinted by permission of Augsburg Fortress, Minneapolis.

As Jacob: Music can be found in *Worship II,* #25.

Once people: From "We Will Never Die," Alexander Solzhenitsyn, translated by Michael Glenny. In *The Oxford Book of Death,* Oxford University Press, New York.

Come, ye: Music can be found in *Worship,* #759.

ALL SOULS

There is a time: From *Siddur Sim Shalom,* a Prayerbook for Shabbat, Festivals, and Weekdays. Edited, with translations, by Rabbi Jules Harlow. Published by The Rabbinical Assembly and The United Synagogue of America. Copyright © 1985, The Rabbinical Assembly. Reprinted by permission of The Rabbinical Assembly.

God redeems: From *Siddur Sim Shalom,* A Prayerbook for Shabbat, Festivals, and Weekdays. Edited, with translations, by Rabbi Jules Harlow. Published by The Rabbinical Assembly and The United Synagogue of America. Copyright © 1985, The Rabbinical Assembly. Reprinted by permission of The Rabbinical Assembly.

Lord Jesus: Excerpts from the English translation of *Order of Christian Funerals* © 1985, International Committee on English in the Liturgy, Inc. (ICEL). All rights reserved.

We still: Quote by Victor J. Schymeinsky. Reprinted by permission of *Maryknoll Magazine* (June 1987), Maryknoll, New York.

Come, brothers and sisters: From "Verses during the Last Kiss: Funeral of the Dead," *Byzantine Daily Worship,* J. Raya, J. de Vinck, Alleluia Press, 1969 and 1988. Used with permission.

The sight: From *Dias de los Muertos (Days of the Dead),* published by the Associates in Multicultural and International Education, Chicago, 1987.

Lord our God: Excerpts from the English translation of *Order of Christian Funerals* © 1985, International Committee on English in the Liturgy, Inc. (ICEL). All rights reserved.

It falsifies: From *For the Life of the World,* Alexander Schmemann. Copyright © 1973, St. Vladimir's Seminary Press, Crestwood. Also published as *The World as Sacrament,* Alexander Schmemann. Copyright © 1966, Darton, Longman and Todd Ltd., London. Used with permission from both publishers.

Let us: Excerpts from the English translation of *Order of Christian Funerals* © 1985, International Committee on English in the Liturgy, Inc. (ICEL). All rights reserved.

And concerning: From the *Revised Standard Version of the Bible.* Copyright © 1946, 1952, 1971 by the Division of Christian Education of the National Council of the Churches of Christ in the U.S.A.. Used with permission.

WILL THE CIRCLE BE UNBROKEN?

Margaret: "Spring and Fall to a Young Child," Gerard Manley Hopkins, in *Poems of Gerard Manley Hopkins,* 4th edition, edited by W. H. Gardner and N. H. MacKenzie. Published by Oxford University Press, New York.

American Indian: From *The Sacred Hoop,* Paula Gunn Allen. Copyright, © 1986, Paula Gunn Allen. Reprinted by permission of Beacon Press, Boston.

The greatest: Excerpt from *Man Is Not Alone* by Abraham Joshua Heschel. Copyright © 1951, Abraham Joshua Heschel, Copyright renewed 1979, Sylvia Heschel. Reprinted by permission of Farrar, Straus and Giroux, Inc.

152   Endnotes

If I die: "Fare well," Frederico Garcia Lorca, in *Selected Poems of Frederico Garcia Lorca,* translated by W. S. Merwin. Copyright © 1955, New Directions Publishing Corporation. Reprinted by permission of New Directions Publishing Corporation. U.S. and Canadian rights.

There is a sense: From *The Meaning of the Sacraments,* Monika Hellwig. Copyright by Monika Hellwig. Used with permission.

Our God, our help: Music can be found in *Worship,* # 579.

Lord, you have: From *The Psalms: A New Translation for Prayer and Worship,* Gary Chamberlain. Copyright © 1984, The Upper Room, Nashville. Used with permission. All rights reserved.

A wisp: From the *Haiku Anthology,* edited by Cor Van den Heuvel. Published by Anchor Press/Doubleday and Co., Inc., New York.

Remember also: From the *Revised Standard Version of the Bible.* Copyright © 1946, 1952, 1971 by the Division of Christian Education of the National Council of the Churches of Christ in the U.S.A. Used with permission.

About suffering: "Musée des Beaux Art," copyright © 1940, renewed 1968 by W. H. Auden. Reprinted from *W. H. Auden Collected Poems,* edited by Edward Mendelson, by permission of Random House, Inc., New York.

Remember, O Lord

The name: At the funeral of Aubry Felix Osborn, priest of Baton Rouge, September 11, 1973.

Cohn said: Excerpt from *God's Grace* by Bernard Malamud. Copyright © 1982, Bernard Malamud. Reprinted by permission of Farrar, Straus and Giroux, Inc., New York.

A priest working: From "Children in El Salvador," Mary Jo Leddy, in the *National Catholic Reporter,* March 17, 1989. Reprinted by permission of *National Catholic Reporter.*

After a dozen: "Poem to My Grandmother in Her Death," Michele Murray, in *The Great Mother and Other Poems.* Copyright © 1974, Sheed and Ward. Used with permission.

Pilgrimage

Shall we gather: Music can be found in *Lead Me, Guide Me,* #103.

Hail, holy: Excerpt from the English translation of *Liturgy of the Hours* © 1974, International Committee on English in the Liturgy, Inc. (ICEL). All rights reserved.

When the Lord: From *The Psalms: A New Translation for Prayer and Worship,* Gary Chamberlain. Copyright © 1984, The Upper Room, Nashville. Used with permission. All rights reserved.

Life be: From *Carmina Gadelica,* vol. 1 by Alexander Carmichael. Reprinted by permission of the Scottish Academic Press Limited.

Our home: Can be found in *The Wisdom of the Saints,* Jill Haak Adels, 1987. Published by Oxford University Press, New York.

I am weak: Music can be found in *Lead Me, Guide Me,* #156

At the Hour of Our Death

Whether [sickness]: From "Rites of Healings: A Reflection in Pastoral Theology," Jennifer Glenn, in *Alternative Futures for Worship,* vol. 7: Anointing of the Sick; volume edited by Peter E. Fink, SJ. Copyright © 1987, The Order of St. Benedict, Inc. Published by The Liturgical Press, Collegeville, Minnesota. Used with permission.

I heard: "I heard a fly buzz when I died" from *The Poems of Emily Dickinson,* edited by Ruth Miller. Copyright © 1968, Ruth Miller Kreisberg. Reprinted by permission of Harper and Row Publishers, Inc., New York.

On the rough: Originally published in *The Partisan Review,* Boston.

Father, you made: Excerpt from *Book of Prayers* © 1982, International Committee on English in the Liturgy, Inc. (ICEL). All rights reserved.

Jesus, Mary: Excerpt from *Book of Prayers* © 1982, International Committee on English in the Liturgy, Inc. (ICEL). All rights reserved.

O God, who broughtest: From *Carmina Gadelica,* vol. 1, Alexander Carmichael. Reprinted by permission of the Scottish Academic Press Limited, Edinburgh, Scotland.

There was once: From "The Man Who Was Aware of Death" in *Tales of the Dervishes,* Idries Shah. Copyright © 1967, Idries Shah. Reprinted by permission of E. P. Dutton, New York.

Professor: From "Aging: A Summing Up and a Letting Go," *Health and Medicine,* vol. 2, no. 4. Publication of the Health and Medicine Policy Research Group, Chicago. Used with permission.

Since in baptism: Excerpts from the English translation of *Order of Christian Funerals* © 1985, International Committee on English in the Liturgy, Inc. (ICEL). All rights reserved.

The embalming: From *Roman Breviary in English* (Autumn), edited by Msgr. Joseph A. Nelson. Copyright © 1950, Benziger Publishing Co., Mission Hills, California.

Formerly, they used: From *The Jewish Catalog.* Copyright © 1973, The Jewish Publication Society of America, Philadelphia.

When life sinks: From the hymn "Confidence," #33, *The Southern Harmony,* published by the University Press of Kentucky, 1987.

I AM NOT RESIGNED

I am not resigned: "Dirge without Music" from *The Buck in the Snow and Other Poems,* Edna St. Vincent Millay. Copyright © 1950, Harper and Brothers. Reprinted by permission of Harper and Row Publishers, Inc., New York.

But it doesn't do: Quoted in Lady Gregory, *Visions and Beliefs in the West of Ireland.*

Every Jew: From *Selected Stores,* by I. L. Peretz, edited by Irving Howe and Eliezer Greenberg. Copyright © 1974, Schocken Books, Inc. Reprinted by permission of Schocken Books, published by Pantheon Books, a division of Random House, Inc.

God did not make: From the *Revised Standard Version Bible,* Copyright © 1946, 1952, 1971 by the Division of Christian Education of the National Council of Churches of Christ in the U.S.A., as emended in the *Lectionary for the Christian People,* copyright © 1986, 1987,

1988 by Pueblo Publishing Company, Inc. Used with permission. All rights reserved.

I can't take: From *An Interrupted Life,* Etty Hillesum. Published by Washington Square Press, 1985.

CONTENDING WITH GOD

Sam/Are you: From *The Trial of God,* by Elie Wiesel, translated by Marion Wiesel. Copyright © 1979, Elirion Associates. Reprinted by permission of Schocken Books, published by Pantheon Books, a division of Random House, Inc.

Lord God, source: Excerpts from the English translation of *Order of Christian Funerals* © 1985, International Committee on English in the Liturgy, Inc. (ICEL). All rights reserved.

Though it may: From *The Cloud of Unknowing,* translated by Clifton Walters. Published by Penguin Books, London, 1961.

Inability: From *Mr. Sammler's Planet,* Saul Bellow. Copyright © 1969, 1970, Saul Bellow. All rights reserved. Reprinted by permission of Viking Penguin, a division of Penguin Books U.S.A. Inc., New York.

In facing: From "The Responsorial Self," Mary Frohlich, in *Liturgy,* March/April 1960. Copyright, The Liturgical Conference, Washington, D.C. All rights reserved. Used with permission.

I LIVE EACH DAY TO KILL DEATH

I am no longer: "I Am No Longer Afraid of Death," Julia Esquivel, *Women in a Changing World,* January 1988. Published by World Council of Churches, New York.

Death is: From *Death by Bread Alone,* Dorothee Soelle, translated by David L. Scheidt. Copyright © 1978, Fortress Press. Reprinted by permission of Augsburg Fortress, Minneapolis.

Franz: From "A Public Witness to Truth," a talk presented for the anniversary of the birth of Franz Jagerstatter by Thomas Gumbleton, published in *The Catholic Worker,* August 1988.

dying is fine: From *Xaipe*, e. e. cummings. Reprinted by permission of the Liveright Publishing Corporation, New York.

Conversion: From *The Call to Conversion: Recovering the Gospel for These Times*, Jim Wallis. Copyright © 1981, Harper and Row Publishers, Inc., New York. Used with permission.

Everything leans: "The Closed Town" from *I Never Saw Another Butterfly*, a collection of children's drawings and poems from Terezin Concentration Camp 1942–1944. Published by McGraw-Hill, 1962. Copyright © 1962, ARTIA Foreign Trade Corporation. Used with permission of Dilia Literary Agency, Czechoslovakia.

The name: Excerpt from *The Second Coming*, Walker Percy. Copyright © 1980, Walker Percy. Reprinted by permission of Farrar, Straus and Giroux, Inc., New York.

I shall die: "Conscientious Objector" from *Collected Lyrics of Edna St. Vincent Millay*. Copyright © 1950, Edna St. Vincent Millay; copyright © renewed 1967, Norma Millay Ellis. Reprinted by permission of Harper and Row Publishers, Inc., New York.

THE LORD IS MY SHEPHERD

The Lord is my: From *The Psalms: A New Translation*. Copyright © 1963, The Grail (England). Used with permission.

Hope is: From *Images of Hope*, William F. Lynch. Published by Helicon Press, Baltimore, 1965.

When the Man: From the *Revised Standard Version Bible*, Copyright © 1946, 1952, 1971 by the Division of Christian Education of the National Council of Churches of Christ in the U.S.A., as emended in the *Lectionary for the Christian People*, copyright © 1986, 1987, 1988 by Pueblo Publishing Company, Inc. Used with permission. All rights reserved.

WHEN YOU FACE OLD AGE

in waiting: From "If You Must Go and I Must Stay," Joyce Carol Oates in *Women Whose Lives Are Food, Men Whose Lives Are Money*. Copyright © 1978, Joyce Carol Oates. Reprinted by permission of Louisiana State University, Baton Rouge.

Dearest Lord: Can be found in *The Oxford Book of Prayer*, edited by George Appleton. Published by Oxford University Press, New York, 1985.

Weaker: "Lebensweisheitspielere," *The Collected Poems of Wallace Stevens*. Copyright © 1952, Wallace Stevens. Reprinted by permission of Alfred A. Knopf, Inc., New York.

Continued life: From *Danglingman*, Saul Bellow. Published by The Vanguard Press, New York, 1944.

Tarrie thou: Can be found in *The Oxford Book of Prayer*, edited by George Appleton. Published by Oxford University Press, New York, 1985.

It is in: "Courage," Anne Sexton, *The Awful Rowing Toward God*. Copyright © 1975, Loring Conant, Jr., Executor of the estate of Anne Sexton. Reprinted by permission of Houghton Mifflin Company, New York.

I know no: From "Aging: A Summing Up and a Letting Go," *Health and Medicine*, vol. 2, no. 4. Publication of the Health and Medicine Policy Research Group, Chicago. Used with permission.

SOME OF THESE MORNINGS

To use fresh: From *In Search of Thérèse*, Patricia O'Connor, in *The Way of the Christian Mystics*, vol. 3, edited by Noel Dermot O'Donoghue. Copyright © 1987, Michael Glazier, Inc. Reprinted with permission from the publisher, Michael Glazier, Inc., Wilmington, Delaware.

Great Spirit: From *Black Elk Speaks*, John G. Neihardt. Copyright © 1932, 1959, 1972, John G. Neihardt. Copyright © 1961, John G. Neihardt Trust. Reprinted by permission of University of Nebraska Press, Lincoln.

Annie folded: From *Annie and The Old One*, Miska Miles. Copyright © 1971, Miska Miles. Reprinted by permission of Little, Brown and Company, Boston.

So Janie: From *Their Eyes Were Watching God,* Zora Neale Hurston. Copyright © 1937, Harper and Brothers; copyright renewed 1965, John C. Hurston and Joel Hurston. Reprinted by permission of Harper and Row Publishers, Inc., New York.

Free at last: Music can be found in *Lead Me, Guide Me,* #293.

Dear Don: From *Pope John XXIII, Shepherd of the Modern World,* Peter Hebblethwaite. Published by Image Books, a division of Doubleday and Company, Inc., Garden City, New York.

For my part: From *Pope John XXIII, Shepherd of the Modern World,* Peter Hebblethwaite. Published by Image Books, a division of Doubleday and Company, Inc., Garden City, New York.

How happy: From *Beethoven,* Maynard Solomon. Copyright © 1977, Schirmer Books, a division of Macmillan Publishing Company. Used with permission.

She hadn't any: From *The Professor's House,* Willa Cather. Published by Random House, Inc., New York.

WHOSE CARE IS WITH THE HUSKS

What will you: "Death Poem," Michele Murray, in *The Great Mother and Other Poems.* Copyright © 1974, Sheed and Ward, Kansas City, Missouri. Used with permission.

In order: From "East Coker" in *Four Quartets.* Copyright © 1943, T. S. Eliot; renewed 1971, Esme Valerie Eliot. Reprinted by permission of Harcourt Brace Jovanovich, Inc., Orlando.

What the world: From *Farming: A Hand Book,* Wendell Berry. Copyright © 1969, Wendell Berry. Reprinted by permission of Harcourt Brace Jovanovich, Inc., Orlando.

The grave: From *The Testament,* Elie Wiesel. Published by Summit Books, New York, 1981.

Everyman: Can be found in *The Oxford Book of Death,* edited by D. J. Enright. Oxford University Press, New York, 1987.

In the Nuremburg: Reprinted with permission of Charles Scribner's Sons, an imprint of Macmillan Publishing Company, from "Born in the Grave" in *The Shaking of the Foundations* by Paul Tillich. Copyright © 1948, Charles Scribner's Sons; copyright renewed © 1976, Hannah Tillich.

Glory, glory: Music can be found in *Lead Me, Guide Me,* #290.

The divine: From *Meditations with Meister Eckhart,* Matthew Fox, Copyright © 1982, Bear and Company, Inc., Sante Fe, New Mexico. Used with permission.

EVERY UNJUST DEATH

Through fields: From "In Chartres," Anne Porter, in *Commonweal,* February 10, 1989. Copyright © 1989, Commonweal Foundation, New York. Used with permission.

And so was he: Can be found in *The Oxford Book of Death,* edited by D. J. Enright. Oxford University Press, New York, 1987.

All of us: Letter to the editor, (Nuclear-Free Takoma Park Committee), Jay Bayerl, *Takoma Park City Newsletter,* October 1988.

The world's: Reprinted with permission of Macmillan Publishing Company from "In Distrust of Merits" in *Collected Poems* by Marianne Moore. Copyright © 1941; renewed 1969, Marianne Moore.

O the night: "O the night of weeping children!" *O The Chimneys,* Nelly Sachs. Translation copyright © 1967, Farrar, Straus and Giroux, Inc., New York.

Although in imagination: From *The Fate of the Earth,* Jonathan Schell. Originally published in *The New Yorker,* February 1, 1982. Copyright © 1982, Jonathan Schell. Reprinted by permission of Alfred A. Knopf, Inc., New York.

I was still: From *Fatal Obsession,* Stephen Greenleaf. Published by Ballantine Books, New York, 1983.

EARTH TO EARTH, ASHES TO ASHES

In the sweat: From the *Revised Standard Version of the Bible.* Copyright © 1946, 1952,

1971 by the Division of Christian Education of the National Council of the Churches of Christ in the U.S.A. Used with permission.

The beautiful: From *American Funeral Customs and the Values of Faith*, Robert W. Hovda. Copyright © 1987, The Order of St. Benedict, Inc. Published by The Liturgical Press, Collegeville, Minnesota. Used with permission.

The words: From the *Revised Standard Version of the Bible*. Copyright © 1946, 1952, 1971 by the Division of Christian Education of the National Council of the Churches of Christ in the U.S.A. Used with permission.

The use of crowns: From *Primitive Christian Symbols*, Jean Daniélou. translated by Donald Attwater. Published by Helicon Press, Baltimore.

O Almighty God: From "The Burial of the Dead: Rite One," in the *Book of Common Prayer*. Published by The Seabury Press, New York. Used with permission.

So we do not: From the *Revised Standard Version Bible*, Copyright © 1946, 1952, 1971 by the Division of Christian Education of the National Council of Churches of Christ in the U.S.A., as emended in the *Lectionary for the Christian People*, copyright © 1986, 1987, 1988 by Pueblo Publishing Company, Inc. Used with permission. All rights reserved.

Because I could: "Because I could not stop for death," *The Poems of Emily Dickinson*, edited by Ruth Miller. Copyright © 1968, Ruth Miller Kreisberg. Reprinted by permission of Harper and Row Publishers, Inc., New York.

SISTER DEATH

I learned: From *A Book of Common Prayer*, Joan Didion. Published by Simon and Schuster, New York, 1977.

O God: Excerpts from the English translation of *Order of Christian Funerals* © 1985, International Committee on English in the Liturgy, Inc. (ICEL). All rights reserved.

Cowards die: From *Julius Caesar*, Act II, Scene ii.

In New Mexico: From "The Kill Hole," Linda Hogan, in *Parabola: Magazine of Myth and*

Tradition, Fall 1988. Reprinted by permission of Linda Hogan.

Bridegroom: From *The Wisdom of the Saints*, Jill Haak Adels. Published by Oxford University Press, New York, 1987.

One might say: From *Death Comes for the Archbishop*. Copyright © 1927, Willa Cather; renewed 1955 by the Executors of the estate of Willa Cather. Reprinted by permission of Alfred A. Knopf, Inc., New York.

Come lovely: From "When Lilacs Last in the Dooryard Bloom'd," Walt Whitman.

If I must: From *Measure for Measure*, Act II, Scene iv.

Blind Francis: From *The Love Letters of Phyllis McGinley*. Copyright 1951, 1952, 1953, 1954 by Phyllis McGinley. Copyright renewed © 1979, 1980, 1981, 1982 by Phyllis Hayden Blake. All rights reserved. Reprinted by permission of Viking Penguin, a division of Penguin Books U.S.A., Inc., New York.

You see the creatures: From *Pilgrim at Tinker Creek*, Annie Dillard. Originally appeared in *Harper's Magazine*. Copyright © 1974, Annie Dillard. Reprinted by permission of the author and her agent, Blanche C. Gregory, Inc.

Steal away: Music can be found in *Lead Me, Guide Me*, #319.

WHERE ARE THE OTHERS?

There is, after all: From an editorial in *Commonweal*, October 21, 1988. Copyright © 1988, Commonweal Foundation. Used with permission.

Touching someone: From "The Laying on of Hands in Healing," Godfrey Diekmann, in *Liturgy*, March/April 1980. Copyright, The Liturgical Conference, Washington, D.C. All rights reserved. Used with permission.

There were some: From "Why Were There so Few?" Elie Wiesel, in *The Courage to Care*, edited by Carol Rittner and Sondra Myers. Copyright © 1986, New York University Press, New York. Used with permission.

But the additional: From *A Visitor From England*, by Anita Brookner. Copyright © 1987, Selobrook, Ltd. Reprinted by permission of

Pantheon Books, a division of Random House, Inc., New York.

I'll be singing: Music can be found in *Lead Me, Guide Me*, #148.

We tried: From the collection of Rabbi Jack Riemer, St. Louis, Missouri.

Those who are dead: From "Breath" ("Souffles") in Birago Diop's *Leurres et Leurres*. Published by *Présence Africaine*, Paris, 1961. Used with permission.

A few light: From *Dubliners* by James Joyce. Copyright © 1916, B. W. Huebsch, Inc. Definitive text copyright © 1967, the estate of James Joyce. All right reserved. Reprinted by permission of Viking Penguin, a division of Penguin Books U.S.A., Inc., New York.

WITH THE DYING

Unfortunately: From *The Meaning of the Sacraments,* Monika Hellwig. Copyright by Monika Hellwig. Used with permission of the author.

Ministering: From "Ministry to Patients with Acquired Immune Deficiency Syndrome: A Spiritual Challenge," Klaus Wendler in *The Journal of Pastoral Care,* 1987. Reprinted with permission of Journal of Pastoral Care Publications, Inc., Myrtle Beach, South Carolina.

What burdens: From *The Optimist's Daughter,* Eudora Welty. Published by Random House, Inc., 1972.

Welcome your servant: Excerpts from the English translation of *Pastoral Care of the Sick: Rites of Anointing and Viaticum* © 1982, International Committee on English in the Liturgy, Inc. (ICEL). All rights reserved.

Every breath: From "There's Life after AIDS, Some Who Have It Say," Michael J. Farrel, in the *National Catholic Reporter,* May 13, 1988. Reprinted by permission of the *National Catholic Reporter,* Kansas City, Missouri.

Here is a man: From *For the Life of the World,* Alexander Schmemann. Copyright © 1973, St. Vladimir's Seminary Press, Crestwood. Also published as *The World as Sacrament,* Alexander Schmemann. Copyright © 1966, Darton, Longman and Todd Ltd., London. Used with permission from both publishers.

Finding this cavern: From the *Haiku Anthology,* edited by Cor Van den Heuvel. Published by Anchor Press/Doubleday and Co., Inc.

Jesus' awareness: From *Homily Service,* Lucy Bregman, March 1989. Copyright, The Liturgical Conference, Washington, D.C. All rights reserved. Used with permission.

Ride on: Music can be found in the *Lutheran Book of Worship,* #121.

Go forth: Excerpts from *Pastoral Care of the Sick: Rites of Anointing and Viaticum* © 1982, International Committee on English in the Liturgy (ICEL). All rights reserved.

WITH THOSE WHO MOURN

It is the will: Homily given by Gerard S. Sloyan at the Mass of Christian burial for J. Sloyan, July 11, 1979.

Nothing can: From *Letters and Papers From Prison,* revised edition, by Dietrich Bonhoeffer. Copyright © 1971, SCM Press, Ltd. Reprinted by permission of Macmillan Publishing Company, New York.

The presence: From a letter after the death of Edna St. Vincent Millay's mother.

We, the rescued: "Chorus of the Rescued," *O The Chimneys,* Nelly Sachs. Translation copyright © 1967, Farrar, Straus and Giroux, Inc. Reprinted by permission of Farrar, Straus and Giroux, Inc., New York.

God of all: Excerpts from the English translation of *Pastoral Care of the Sick: Rites of Anointing and Viaticum* © 1982, International Committee on English in the Liturgy, Inc. (ICEL). All rights reserved.

You are the author: Excerpts from the English translation of *Order of Christian Funerals* © 1985, International Committee on English in the Liturgy, Inc. (ICEL). All rights reserved.

One may know: From *Adam, Eve and the Serpent: Changing Patterns of Sexual Morality,* Elaine Pagels. Copyright © 1988, Elaine Pagels. Reprinted by permission of Random House, Inc., New York.

Lord, N. is gone: Excerpts from the English translation of *Order of Christian Funerals*

© 1985, International Committee on English in the Liturgy, Inc. (ICEL).

If thou didst: From *Hamlet,* Act V, Scene ii.

May the love: Excerpts from the English translation of *Order of Christian Funerals* © 1985, International Committee on English in the Liturgy, Inc. (ICEL).

Being a widow: From *Widow,* Lynn Caine. Published by Bantam Books, New York, 1987.

In the earliest: From a homily by Gerard S. Sloyan at the Mass of Christian burial for John Maloney, January 2, 1989.

THE BOSOM OF ABRAHAM

Death blessings: From *Carmina Gadelica,* vol. 1, Alexander Carmichael. Reprinted by permission of the Scottish Academic Press Limited, Edinburgh, Scotland.

On the day: From *Consecration/Dedication Sundays.* Text from the Maronite Liturgy printed with permission of the Diocese of St. Marion-U.S.A.

To you, O Lord: Excerpts from the English translation of *Order of Christian Funerals* © 1985, International Committee on English in the Liturgy, Inc. (ICEL).

Into your hands: Excerpts from the English translation of *Order of Christian Funerals* © 1985, International Committee on English in the Liturgy, Inc. (ICEL).

IN MY FLESH I SHALL SEE GOD

I know: Excerpts from the English translation of *Order of Christian Funerals* © 1985, International Committee on English in the Liturgy, Inc. (ICEL).

God of loving: Excerpts from the English translation of *Order of Christian Funerals* © 1985, International Committee on English in the Liturgy, Inc. (ICEL).

Standing by: "The Moment," Patricia Hampl. Originally published in *The New Yorker,* December 16, 1986. Copyright © 1986, Patricia Hampl. Used with permission.

Let us observe: From "First Epistle to the Corinthians," *The Early Christian Fathers.*

MERCY

Surely God: From *The Psalms: A New Translation for Prayer and Worship,* Gary Chamberlain. Copyright © 1984, The Upper Room, Nashville. Used with permission.

Mr. Head: Excerpt from "The Artificial Nigger," *A Good Man is Hard to Find and Other Stories.* Copyright © 1955, Flannery O'Connor; renewed 1983, Regina O'Connor. Reprinted by permission of Harcourt Brace Jovanovich, Inc., Orlando.

God, lover of souls: Excerpts from the English translation of *Order of Christian Funerals* © 1985, International Committee on English in the Liturgy, Inc. (ICEL).

Lord Jesus, our Redeemer: Excerpts from the English translation of *Order of Christian Funerals* © 1985, International Committee on English in the Liturgy, Inc. (ICEL).

CHRIST, WHO CLAIMED YOU IN BAPTISM

You have become: Excerpts from the *Rite of Christian Initiation of Adults* © 1985, International Committee on English in the Liturgy, Inc. (ICEL).

You have been: Excerpts from the *Rite of Christian Initiation of Adults* © 1985, International Committee on English in the Liturgy, Inc. (ICEL).

God has made: From *Documents of the Baptismal Liturgy,* E. C. Whitaker. Published by the Society for Promoting Christian Knowledge, London, 1977.

We now find: From a talk given by Aidan Kavanagh at the convocation of the North American Forum on the Catechumenate in Washington, September 12, 1987. Used with permission.

The primary: From "Biblical Images of Water," Irene Nowell, in *Liturgy,* Summer 1987. Copyright, The Liturgical Conference, Washington, D.C. All rights reserved. Used with permission.

ALL WE GO DOWN TO THE DUST: ALLELUIA

Give rest: "Contakion of the Departed," anonymous. From *The Harper Book of Christian Poetry*, selected and introduced by Anthony S. Mercatante. Copyright © 1972, Anthony S. Mercatante. Published by Harper and Row Publishers, Inc. Used with permission.

Paschal mystery: From *The Death of a Christian: The Rite of Funerals*. Copyright © 1980, Pueblo Publishing Company, Inc., New York. Used with permission.

How often: From a homily prepared for the meeting of the Federation of Diocesan Liturgical Commissions, San Diego, October 1988.

And thou, Jesus: Can be found in *Women's Prayer Services*, edited by Iben Gjerding and Katherine Kinnamon. Published by Twenty-Third Publications, Mystic, Connecticut.

What Thérèse: From *In Search of Thérèse*, Patricia O'Connor, in *The Way of the Christian Mystics*, vol. 3, edited by Noel Dermot O'Donoghue. Copyright © 1987, Michael Glazier, Inc. Reprinted by permission of Michael Glazier, Inc., Wilmington, Delaware.

It would be: From *For the Life of the World*, Alexander Schmemann. Copyright © 1973, St. Vladimir's Seminary Press, Crestwood. Also published as *The World as Sacrament*, Alexander Schmemann. Copyright © 1966, Darton, Longman and Todd Ltd., London. Used with permission from both publishers.

Nearer, my God: Music can be found in *Lead Me, Guide Me*, #143.

HE DESCENDED TO THE DEAD

O deathless: Can be found in the *Byzantine Book of Hours*.

Almighty God: Excerpts from the English translation of *Order of Christian Funerals*

© 1985, International Committee on English in the Liturgy, Inc. (ICEL). All rights reserved.

In speaking: From *Early Syriac Theology*, Msgr. Seely J. Beggiani. Copyright © 1983, University Press of America, Inc., Lanham, Maryland. Used with permission.

COMMITTAL

In sure and certain: From "Burial of the Dead: Rite One, The Commital" in *The Book of Common Prayer*. Published by The Seabury Press, New York. Used with permission.

The old men: "The Old Men Used to Sing," from *Revolutionary Petunias and Other Poems*. Copyright © 1970, Alice Walker. Reprinted by permission of Harcourt Brace Jovanovich, Inc., Orlando.

All praise: Excerpts from the English translation of *Order of Christian Funerals* © 1985, International Committee on English in the Liturgy, Inc. (ICEL). All rights reserved.

IF I DIE BEFORE I WAKE

May God open: From *Celtic Prayers*, selected by Avery Brooks, from the collection of Alexander Carmichael. Copyright © 1981, The Seabury Press, New York. Used with permission.

In thy name: From *Celtic Prayers*, selected by Avery Brooks, from the collection of Alexander Carmichael. Copyright © 1981, The Seabury Press, New York. Used with permission.

The eighteenth-century: From *Teaching a Stone to Talk*. Copyright © 1982, Annie Dillard. Reprinted by permission of Harper and Row Publishers, Inc., New York.

However blind: From *The Needs of Strangers* by Michael Ignatieff. Copyright © 1984, Michael Ignatieff. All rights reserved. Reprinted by permission of Viking Penguin, a division of Penguin Books U.S.A. Inc., New York.

God be in my hede: "Hymnus," *The Cherry Tree*, a collection of poems chosen by Geoffrey Grigson. Copyright © 1959, Geoffrey Grigson. Published by The Vanguard Press, Inc.

O God, whose days: From "Burial of the Dead: Rite Two," in *The Book of Common Prayer.* Published by The Seabury Press, New York. Used with permission.

The day is past: From the hymn "Evening Shade", #46, in the 1987 edition of *The Southern Harmony* published by the University Press of Kentucky, Lexington.

DIES IRAE

Hear'st thou: "Dies Irae," translated by Richard Crashaw, in *The Harper Book of Christian Poetry,* selected and introduced by Anthony S. Mercatante. Copyright © 1972, Anthony S. Mercatante. Published by Harper and Row Publishers, Inc. Used with permission.

Before his death: From "The Query of Queries," in *Tales of the Hasidim: The Early Masters,* Martin Buber. Copyright © 1947, Martin Buber; renewed 1975, Schocken Books, Inc. Published by Pantheon Books, a division of Random House, Inc., New York.

If ever: Excerpted from *The Book of Job,* translated by Stephen Mitchell. Copyright © 1987, Stephen Mitchell. Published by North Point Press, Berkeley. Used with permission.

This ae night: "A Lyke-Wake Dirge," *The Cherry Tree,* a collection of poems chosen by Geoffrey Grigson. Copyright © 1959, Geoffrey Grigson. Published by The Vanguard Press, Inc., New York.

COME, LORD JESUS

Remember, Lord: From *Come, Lord Jesus,* Lucien Deiss. Copyright © 1976, 1981, Lucien Deiss. Published by World Library Publications, Inc., Schiller Park, Illinois. All rights reserved. Used with permission.

We are much: From *Letters and Papers From Prison,* revised edition, by Dietrich Bonhoeffer. Copyright © 1971, SCM Press, Ltd. Reprinted by permission of Macmillan Publishing Company, New York.

Come, my Lord: Reprinted from *The Weather of the Heart* by Madeleine L'Engle. Copyright © 1978, Crosswicke. Used by permission of Harold Shaw Publishers, Wheaton, Illinois.

I heard Death: From Nisibene Hymns, #52, St. Ephrem, in *Harp of the Spirit,* edited and translated by Sebastian Grock. Copyright, The Fellowship of St. Alban and St. Sergius, London. Used with permission.

Oh, when I come: "Give Me Jesus" from *The Harper Book of Christian Poetry,* selected and introduced by Anthony S. Mercatante. Copyright © 1972, Anthony S. Mercatante. Published by Harper and Row Publishers, Inc., New York. Used with permission.

My purity: "Antiphon," Methodius of Olympus, in *Early Christian Prayers,* edited by A. Hammon, English translation by Walter Mitchell. Copyright © 1961 by H. Regnery Co. All rights reserved. Reprinted by special permission from Regnery Gateway, Inc., Washington, D.C.

IN PARADISUM

The body's: From "Conscious of Our Need," Rachel Reeder, in *Liturgy,* Winter 1987. Copyright, The Liturgical Conference, Washington, D.C. All rights reserved. Used with permission.

We must stop: From "Aging: A Summing Up and a Letting Go," *Health and Medicine,* vol. 2, no. 4. Publication of the Health and Medicine Policy Research Group, Chicago. Used with permission.

Deep river: Music can be found in *Lead Me, Guide Me,* #150.

Fix me: Music can be found in *Songs of Zion,* #122.

Light's abode: "The Church Triumphant," translated by John Mason Neale, altered. Music can be found in *The Hymnal,* #621.

I looked over: Music can be found in *Lead Me, Guide Me,* #147.

Into your hands: Excerpts from the English translation of *Order of Christian Funerals* © 1985, International Committee on English in the Liturgy, Inc. (ICEL). All rights reserved.